TELL ME, PRETTY MAIDEN

TELL ME, PRETTY MAIDEN

THE VICTORIAN and EDWARDIAN NUDE

RONALD PEARSALL

Grange
BOOKS

Published by Grange Books
An Imprint of Books & Toys Limited
The Grange
Grange Yard
LONDON   SE1   3AG

ISBN: 1·85627·235·4

This edition published 1992
Printed by: Gráficas Reunidas, S.A. (Madrid)

Copyright © Webb & Bower (Publishers) Limited
1981

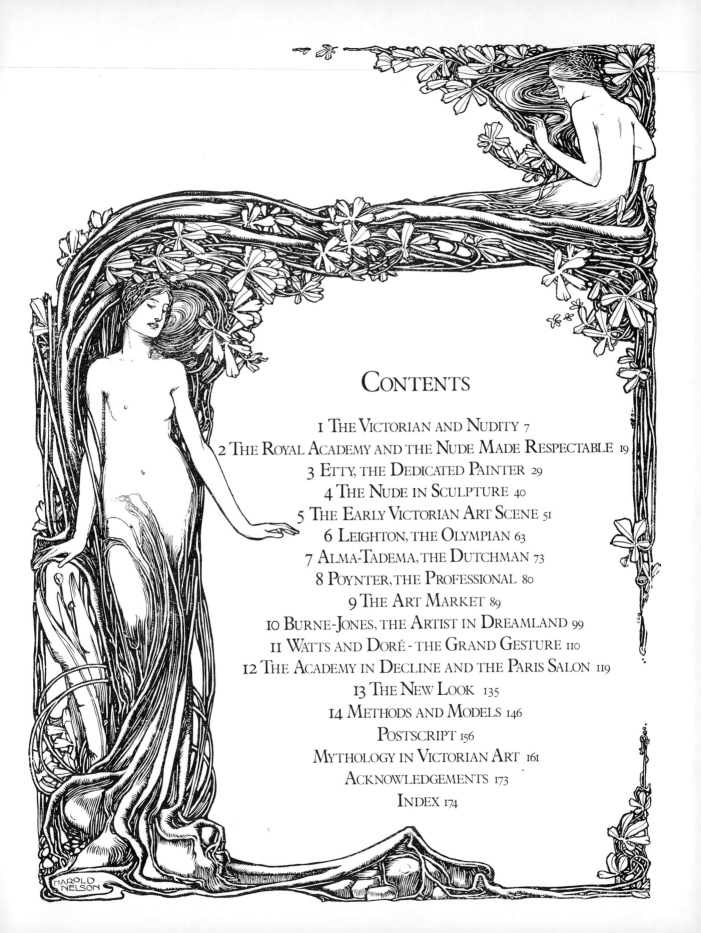

CONTENTS

HAROLD
NELSON

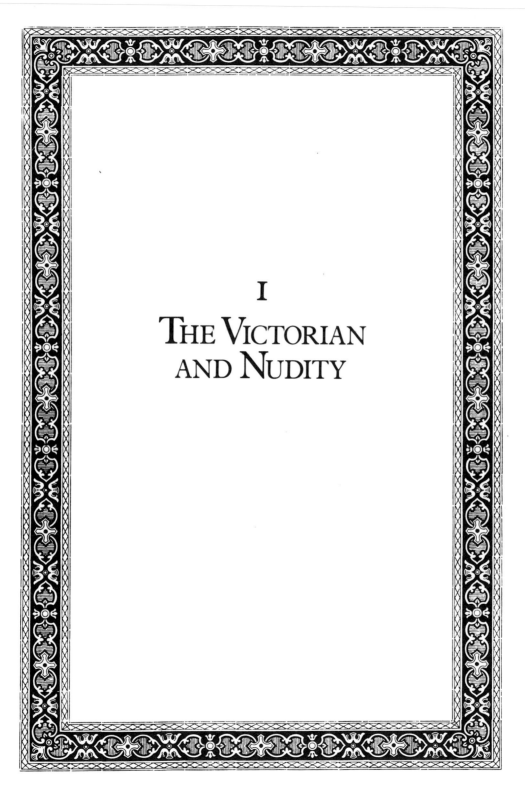

I
THE VICTORIAN
AND NUDITY

What did the Victorians think about nudity? This depended largely on who they were, and where they were. The bathing machines at the seaside, hauled in and out of the water by horses, are often supposed to be representative of respectability at its primmest, disgorging men and women in bathing costumes hardly more revealing than everyday dress. Not many people realized, however, that the bathers often went in naked. The novelist George Meredith wrote to his friend, the lawyer William Hardman, of his observations at Eastbourne, where 'antique virgins, spy-glass in hand' watched naked men scampering in and out of their bathing machines.

Francis Kilvert, a clergyman whose diaries give a colourful picture of Victorian life as it was, visited Seaton in Devon, and saw the girls with 'shoes, stockings, and drawers off wading in the tide, holding up their clothes nearly to the waist and naked from the waist downwards'. On secluded beaches, nudists enjoyed what was described as the 'air bath' and the ponds on Hampstead Heath were regularly used by naked swimmers. Nudists, later to be called naturists, were permitted in selected situations, provided that no one spoke of them or drew attention to them as startling examples of depravity.

Although nude bathing was long established from the eighteenth century and had not provoked much attention, there were always, of course, people who spoke against it. To many nude bathing ran totally counter to respectability and modesty. In 1860 a Dr Thompson wrote a book called *Health Resorts of Great Britain* and drew attention to the heinous conditions prevailing at Ramsgate, where 'both modesty and manners seem to be left at the lodging, so that the bathers on the one hand, and the line of lookers-on, on the other, seem to have no more sense of decency than so many South Sea Islanders'. Nor were men the chief offenders. Dr Thompson wrote severely of the 'unblushing intrusiveness of the fair sex'.

There was an answer. Male bathers should be compelled to wear short drawers, which did not in the least 'impede the movement of the body'. Specific legislation was not passed, much as this would have been welcomed by those most shocked, but there were ample laws to cover the situation, from those against committing a public nuisance upwards.

Letters to *The Times* often reflect attacks of moral indignation. In 1856 'A Father of a Family at Present at Margate' made a personal plea to the editor:

With a few strokes of your powerful pen you may do much for the cause of morality. If you were here the indecent and disgusting exhibitions which take place on the Marine Parade would shock you, as it must everyone not lost to common decency and propriety. I shall say no more but many families will bear me out in my statement if necessary.

Further correspondence ensued. 'Large numbers of ladies spend their mornings in close proximity to scores of naked men,' one writer noted. There was only one

Opposite Women do not change much over the centuries in their vital statistics, and this photograph represents an agreeable norm. Throughout the Victorian period painters tried to refine the image, often enhancing the sexual overtones despite themselves.

The Victorian women were obsessed with the tiny waist, which drew attention to the hips and the breasts. The corset also acted as an anchor for one of the most important erotic accessories of the late nineteenth century—the suspender.

hypothesis that would be acceptable—that the women were 'artists and that they are studying from the life'. It was all 'abominable and ought to be abated'. If there was a Society for the Suppression of Vice, there was 'ample scope for its exertions'.

There *was* a Society for the Suppression of Vice. It had been formed in 1802, and its secretary had promised a holy war against profanation of Sunday, blasphemous publications, obscene books and prints, brothels and, rather tamely, fortune-tellers. The Society was a spin-off from the fervent evangelical movements of the time, when children were told that they would burn eternally in hell if they did not behave themselves. Its first committee included the Rev. Thomas Bowdler, in 1818 to produce his 'Family Shakespeare' in which every dubious act or word was expunged, though he left the violence alone. Violence, in his opinion, did not corrupt or offend anyone's code of morals.

The Society for the Suppression of Vice was never as powerful as it pretended to be, though it often had the support of magistrates. Its main target was pornography, and after the Napoleonic Wars there was plenty of that about, for peace brought a great invasion of French prostitutes, who set themselves up in Leicester Square, Waterloo Place and Regent Street, and attracted the supposed wrath of the editor of the scurrilous weekly magazine *The Town*.

> If the police were to search the lodgings of these filthy French harlots they would find prints of the most horrible description, and paintings unmatched for bestiality. These diabolical incitements to venery are, and we trust always will be, *foreign* to Englishmen.

In this, he was in error. The London of the Regency had an army of prostitutes with a repertoire of wiles and tricks unparalleled in Europe. Those at the top end of the market were widely cultivated by the friends and acquaintances of the man who set the tone of the upper classes, the Prince Regent, later George IV.

Throughout the Victorian period there were greater numbers of prostitutes in London, and Henry Mayhew, who can be considered the first social historian with his massive *London Labour and the London Poor* (1851–62), estimated their numbers at 80,000 in London alone. It was the shadow side of Victorian life and, compared with this, nude bathing at the seaside was hardly worth mentioning.

Nudity in private was surprisingly a totally different matter. Many married women boasted proudly that their husbands had never seen them naked. Women in childbirth were often smothered with voluminous clothing, modesty being more important than commonsense. Midwives, despite the term, were often male, and often had to carry out their duties in darkened rooms, as if the woman's sense of decorum was better preserved.

Advanced educationalists of the nineteenth century thought that children at school should be shown photographs of the nude in ancient sculpture so that they could become 'immunized'. It was also suggested that photographs of nude men and women should be shown to the children. It is impossible to say whether this project was ever carried out, though the odds are against it—exposure to the nude would result in sexual experiment and Bacchanalian fury, to the ruin of civilization.

The Victorians were breast-orientated. The women were caught between modesty and the instinctive desire to make themselves sexually interesting objects.

Erotica of all kinds was a secret underground industry, but
some idea of its scope can be seen from this advertisement.
Holywell Street was the centre of the dirty book trade, and
was swept away in Edwardian times when the Aldwych and
Kingsway were driven through the slums.

Cleavage, even amongst the most respectable, could reach almost to the waist, and exposure of the upper part of the breasts was the rule rather than the exception, provided that the nipples were covered, though they could be hinted at. Uplift was provided not by brassières, but corsets, which pushed the breasts up into the likeness of a pair of melons. (Where breasts were ample, cleavage was almost lost, and the nearest analogy could then be a bolster.) The poet Robert Browning spoke of this when he wrote about 'the breast's superb abundance where a man may lay his head'. Those women with small breasts were at a disadvantage, and took to wearing padding. A camisole-like article was produced in which whalebone and wire springs were built in to augment any slight protuberances.

The brassière was not known in Britain until 1907 when *Vogue* mentioned it, and when it did arrive about 1912 it was called a bust corset. The brassière was particularly popular in the United States, where Mary Phelps Jacob introduced in 1913 a model which was soft, short, with separate breasts, and was named the Backless Bra.

Corsets existed in a variety of types, some of them cunningly made to make the best of sagging or insignificant breasts. Young girls were forced to wear them long before there was any sign of budding womanhood, for they—and their mothers—probably believed that the reason for the corset was to produce the desirable small waist. The corset was often worn twenty-four hours a day, even in bed, and, reported the *Englishwoman's Domestic Magazine*, 'carries no hardship beyond an occasional fainting fit'.

The ideal vital statistics of 1890 make interesting reading: waist 22 inches, bust 36 inches, hips 40 inches. From the evidence of paper patterns it is clear that these figures were too ambitious. The average woman had a larger waist and a smaller bust—if there was an average woman. The rich ate too much so they were more likely to be fat, and the poor ate too little so they were more likely to be thin. Many fashion-conscious women set themselves a target of an 18-inch waist. Intrigued by this, several historians of fashion have made searching enquiries to see if anyone actually made it, by examining the costumes in museums throughout the country. They are unanimous in the opinion that the 18-inch waist was a myth.

Despite the acceptance of the breasts as a desirable womanly property, no such latitude was extended towards the legs. These were always, theoretically, to be covered, and a glimpse of ankle and calf was, hopefully, the most that could be seen, perhaps just as well, as until the last half of the century drawers were not worn. They were regarded as only fit to be worn by prostitutes and ballet dancers (who were often grouped together). While it was more difficult for legs to be seen, when they were observed there was a good deal more to see, and not surprisingly voyeurism was a popular Victorian pastime.

In the 1850s the crinoline dominated women's fashions. The crinoline was an enormous billowing hoop, which gave women the appearance of a pin-cushion. The struts of the crinoline were made of whalebone and sprung steel, and over the hoop were voluminous petticoats. The crinoline was in a constant state of movement, swaying from side to side, and any pressure on the hoops would cause the other side of the crinoline to spring up. All this was very intriguing to men, and the editor of *Punch* considered printing a joke on the subject, rejecting it when it seemed risky:

Why may the crinoline be justly regarded as a social invention?
Because it enables us to see more of our friends than we used to.

An amusing court case occurred in 1853 when Mrs Lowe of Victoria Grove, Kensington, was charged with permitting her female servant 'to stand on the sill of an upstairs window, in order to clean it, whereby the life of the servant was endangered and the public decency shocked'.

When drawers were worn, they were 'split drawers', two legs joined together with tapes. A pair of Queen Victoria's split drawers was sold at auction a few years ago, vast and uncompromising. The first reference to knickers seems to have been in *Cassell's Magazine* in the 1880s, when flannel knickers were recommended in preference to flannel petticoats, though twenty years later during the Edwardian period all sorts of exotic materials were used, including silk and satin.

Although the very word leg was enough to throw a virtuous maiden into a tizzy, and was substituted by the word limb or the curious term 'unmentionable', women had no objections to wearing coloured stockings. If legs were seen (horrid

The nearly-nude as an aid to commerce. Setting the figure in
a vaguely classical background and providing her with
imitation Greek drapery helped to deter criticism. The
inclusion of doves also adds to the general scheme.

This advertisement followed the previous one a fortnight
later—identical except for the fact that the draperies now
cover the breasts. An interesting example showing that
Victorian pressures were not yet dead.

thought) it would no doubt be safer to have them encased. On the other hand, if a naked leg was erotic in the extreme, if a stockinged leg was provocative but not actually criminal, a stocking coming down and collecting in folds around an attractive ankle was, tragedy upon tragedy, embarrassing and unbecoming.

The suspender was invented to cope with this contingency. The suspender was a separate harness, and was later worn over the corset. Not until the Edwardian age was it attached to the corset. In 1876 French dancers in an Offenbach *opéra bouffe* at the Alhambra Theatre, Leicester Square, caused a stir by their display of suspenders. Observers talked with awe of their 'naked thighs with suspenders stretched across them to keep up the stockings'. Shocking as the spectacle was, suspenders had become commonplace by 1878, to create a new erotic garment.

The cult of the leg, in fact, was being relentlessly promoted by French dancers and actresses. The cancan was first danced on the English stage in 1867 by a Creole woman known as Finette, who had been Whistler's mistress. The dance had been known in France for several decades, since the 1830s, and had been stigmatized by the German poet Heine as a symptom of social disillusion. In Britain it was seen as the first sign of decadence. *The Times* did not approve but not surprisingly the Prince of Wales, who was in the audience, did. In 1874 a dance called the ripirelle was performed at the St James's Theatre. The critic of the magazine *Vanity Fair* did not like it, and said so, and the proprietor was sued for libel. The ripirelle was, he said, 'simply a cancan with all the indecency and none of the art of the original'. He called the Lord Chamberlain as witness, and the Lord Chamberlain agreed with him. Cancans and cancan-type dances were banned. Men who liked to look at ladies' legs with or without suspenders were disappointed. They had to go elsewhere.

Very popular with men-about-town were *Tableaux Vivants* (living pictures), in which unclothed and partly clothed women posed, illustrating some theme of no great consequence, a kind of waxwork show. The protagonists often wore skin-coloured costumes to deceive the customers, and although in some of the clubs the women were naked *Tableaux Vivants* were largely innocuous. The only kind of woman who could be put on display stripped to the waist was a black woman, and black women were often put on show as part of an exhibition glorifying the Empire. They were also photographed, and were the only naked-from-the-waist-up women to receive exposure in respectable magazines.

Although the opera was a popular Victorian art form, well-bred girls were not allowed to attend if there was a ballet. The costume of classical ballet, a type of entertainment appreciated by all classes owing to the eminence of the great ballerina Taglioni, was held to be too provocative. But men and women, anxious to see naked people whether from curiosity or the desire to be sexually aroused, had only to turn into the nearest art gallery to see pictures which, if they were shown outside in the street, would result in prosecution under the Obscene Publications Act of 1857.

Paintings of the nude in galleries were beyond criticism, and beyond prosecution. The reason for this makes a fascinating story.

Venus and Cupid by Etty. This picture shows clearly why
many acute observers classed Etty with the great Italian
painters of the past. Etty was never afraid to use dramatic
colour, and his skin tones have a vibrancy rare in art of all
ages and exceptional during the nineteenth century.

Once again in this study of two women Etty poses his nudes
against a crimson cloth. It is interesting to compare his
treatment of floating draperies with that of Lord Leighton
or Watts.

2
THE ROYAL ACADEMY
AND THE NUDE
MADE RESPECTABLE

In 1769 with 136 works the Royal Academy held its first exhibition in rooms in Pall Mall. For more than 150 years it was the main showplace of British art. During this time there was a great market for contemporary art, for there was a good deal of new money in Great Britain. Other people besides the aristocracy were looking for pictures to decorate their houses, people who came unprejudiced to pictures and did not like what were referred to as the 'Black Masters'—the great paintings of the past often barely seen beneath heavy coats of dark varnish.

These new buyers liked picturesque paintings, portraits and pictures that told a story with as much detail as possible. There was a great industry in supplying portraits, and three of the leading artists in this field were Reynolds (1723–92), Romney (1734–1802) and Gainsborough (1727–88). Sir Joshua Reynolds could do a face in a day, finishing the rest of the picture in his studio, and until 1800 averaged £210 a picture, with smaller ones a quarter of this. Thomas Gainsborough, who today is valued far higher, was up to £168 a picture, while Romney was in a slightly lower league at £105 a picture. At a time when the average family income was well under £100 a year these were considerable sums of money, but as the nineteenth century progressed these portraits were sold and resold at huge prices, culminating in 1926 when a Romney portrait was sold for £46,200.

Those pictures which told a story, however, were the most popular among ordinary folk and in 1811 Benjamin West sold his painting of *Christ Healing the Sick* for £3,150—with one exception the highest fee paid before 1860. There was also a profitable spin-off in engravings: 840 different versions of this picture appeared as engravings, some of them retailing for as much as £5. There was also a considerable amount of money to be made by exhibiting these huge and densely detailed pictures, and one painting, *Death of Chatham* by the American artist John Copley, exhibited in 1779–80, made £5,000 in 'gate money' alone. It was the skill and expertise of the artist that people came along to gape and marvel at.

If the painter provided what the rich or the general public wanted there was no end to the rewards, either monetary or in the form of knighthoods, but those who miscalculated the taste of the time could come to a sad end. Typical of these was Francis Danby, whose painting *The Deluge* was contemptuously described as 'an unforgettable salad of clammy nude bodies'. Danby had come to London from Ireland in 1813, lived for a time in Wales and in Switzerland, and ended up in squalor with ten children, three by his mistress, and seven by his wife.

The themes for paintings in the late eighteenth and early nineteenth centuries were largely taken from religion or recent history, but in 1800 a new source of inspiration was uncovered—although to begin with no one recognized it as such.

British collectors and enthusiasts at that time were ransacking Europe of its treasures, especially its paintings. Agents were permanently employed in countries such as Italy to buy pictures for their employers and ship them back to England. Not surprisingly there was a good deal of faking and double-dealing going on at all levels and, for example, there were factories in London which, by baking paintings in ovens to reproduce the effects of time, provided 'old masters' at a fraction of the cost of genuine ones.

One of these enthusiasts was Thomas Bruce, seventh Earl of Elgin, who in 1800 was visiting Athens with the aim of taking casts or making drawings of the remains of the Greek sculptures on the Parthenon. Athens had been bombarded by

This fairy painting attributed to Daniel Maclise (1806–70) is
saved from indecorum by the pretence that the women
depicted are not real women. A degree of incompetence also
helps to dispel suspicion. Maclise is best known as a painter
of historical and Shakespearean subjects.

Venetian warships, hits had been scored on the Parthenon and Greece was occupied
by the Turks, who were Britain's allies in the Napoleonic Wars. As the Parthenon
was providing a convenient quarry for building material, and therefore was not
likely to last as it was for any length of time, the Earl of Elgin decided that it would
not be considered reprehensible actually to take the sculptures back to England—
which he did, at a cost of £70,000.

On his way back he stopped off in Paris, where he was arrested and detained for
three years, but eventually the sculptures from the Parthenon were put on show in
his house in Park Lane and opened to visitors in 1807. British artists and sculptors

came to marvel at these battered and fragmentary figures, and although the collection was valued by the London connoisseur Richard Payne Knight at £25,000, hardly more than a third of the cost of bringing them to Britain from Greece, the art world considered that the Earl of Elgin had performed a noble act in rescuing the marbles from neglect, and for persevering when the ship carrying them was wrecked and the marbles were recovered from the sea. The British government bought them from Elgin for £35,000, and they were placed in the British Museum in 1816, where they have remained to this day (to the puzzlement of thousands of visitors who fail to see any beauty in mangled and broken statues).

However, the Elgin Marbles created great interest, and there was a fashion for anything Greek. Women took to wearing clothes in the Greek style, and architecture was strongly influenced, as we can still see in the giant caryatids— standing female figures—of St Pancras Church.

Of course, there were other examples of antique sculpture in existence, and one of the best known was the Apollo Belvedere, discovered at Antium in Italy in 1503 and purchased by Pope Julius II, who placed it in the Vatican. There was also the Medici Venus, found near Tivoli, and removed to France in 1680. It had however lost a hand, and this unfortunately had been restored at too sharp an angle.

In 1820 the most famous statue in the world was discovered—the Venus de Milo. It was placed on show in the Louvre in 1834 and until 1893 was believed to be of the fifth century BC, and the only statue from that period with a head left intact. Later scholarship put the date at about 100 BC, which, while making it less interesting to specialists, made no difference to its popularity.

From the first, the Venus de Milo was regarded as a great masterpiece, except by those who saw in its semi-nakedness something improper. There was little that the prudish could do. The acceptance of Greek nude statues as great art made it almost impossible to carry out a campaign against them, and throughout the nineteenth century the nude in art was reluctantly accepted—if it was served up in a religious, classical or mythological setting.

The nudity of Greek statuary however should not lead us to believe that in the day-to-day business of life men and women in classical times carried out their duties unclothed, though certainly in competitions the participants were naked, taking pride in the beauty of their bodies. The men were more likely to be naked than women, who were usually lightly clothed, for in a society which accepted homosexuality there was no embarrassment in this.

The Romans on the other hand were shocked by nakedness, which they equated with decadence, and if they were naked it was with some practical purpose, such as bathing. In Byzantine art too, for fear of idolatry, the nude disappears, and in the early years of Christianity the nude was looked upon as a symbol of pagan times, illustrative of humiliation and shame. However, any paintings of Jesus Christ had to depict him partly naked, especially in such episodes as the flagellation, the crucifixion and the entombment, and the Church was obliged to come to terms with this.

There were other Biblical events which clashed with the mediaeval reluctance to depict nudes, the most obvious being Adam and Eve, but in general all scenes which involved humiliation, martyrdom and torture taxed the sensibilities of the artist—not to mention his technique. In an effort—almost always successful—to

The Expulsion of Adam and Eve from the Garden of Eden by
John Faed (1819–1902), elected Associate of the Royal
Scottish Academy in 1847. The subject made it respectable,
for no one could deny that Adam and Eve were sent naked
into the wilderness.

desexualize, Adams and Eves are crude and stodgy, but artists were faced with an additional problem when theologians in the thirteenth century decided that in the Resurrection the bodies emerging from their graves would not only be naked, but also perfect. After many hundreds of years, the body beautiful needed to be rediscovered.

Real people do not change enormously over the centuries, but artists' conceptions of the ideal do. To the Greeks, the formula was simple: in a female nude the distance between breasts, the distance between the lower breast and the navel and the distance between the navel and the division of the legs, should be the same and the head should be approximately an eighth of the length of the figure. The important features of the female nude were the swell of the breast and the curve of the hip. Ribs and muscles were important, and were to be depicted naturalistically.

This shape did not appeal to artists and sculptors in the Middle Ages. They wished to fit woman into a geometrical pattern, and did not see the hips and breasts as the important zones. Their ideal woman had an elongated oval stomach occupying much of the torso, surmounted by two small hemispheres, and these tastes were reflected in fashion of the period. There was no depiction of ribs or muscles, and for a considerable time this interpretation of the nude woman held sway, against all the evidence of the senses. Nevertheless, the artists *could* depict what they saw very accurately, as proved by their lively animals and birds.

When artists realized that they did not have to fit their women into a ridiculous pattern and could paint what they saw, nude painting changed, as exemplified by Sebastiano del Piombo (1485–1547), and his long-armed wide-hipped statuesque women. The life drawings of Sebastiano del Piombo are the earliest sketches from the nude figure which have come down to us. However, although he and his contemporaries differed in their preferences, their pictures largely conform to the ideal set out by the Greeks.

The delicacy of Botticelli and the exuberance of Raphael lead us to the gusto of Rubens who in contrast threw all notions of ideal beauty to the wind and painted fat naked women. Almost contemporary with Raphael was Cranach (1472–1553), who also created a type of his own with narrow shoulders and long languorous legs, small breasts and a narrow waist. He was one of the first painters since the Middle Ages to be openly erotic, even when dealing with religious themes. During this period nudes begin to appear in books as, for example, decoration in the *New Testament* of Erasmus (1519).

Rembrandt (1606–69) painted and drew ugly fat naked women with truth and compassion, but it was the French who evolved the chic and sensual nude, preferably petite and vulnerable, and—a pose that once symbolized lust—from the back. François Boucher (1703–70) was the key painter of prettiness, and although he sometimes set his bewitching creatures against a mythological background they are clearly the young women of eighteenth-century France flaunting their charms. Boucher was painter to King Louis XV, and his acceptance by the Court was to play an important role in the greater freedom given to painters of the nude in France than was the case with their English counterparts. Several Boucher paintings found their way into the hands of the fourth Marquis of Hertford who, dying unmarried in 1870, left his great wealth and priceless art collection to his alleged half-brother, Sir

Another treatment of Adam and Eve, this time by Gustave
Doré (1833–83). Doré specialized in writhing nude bodies,
and here he is unusually decorous, even providing Eve with
a shrub as modest covering.

Richard Wallace (thus the Wallace Collection, bequeathed to the British nation in 1897).

There was no strict prohibition of the painting of nudes in England while Boucher was so active in France, but there was certainly no delight in the naked female form as something purely sensuous. William Blake (1757–1827) painted male and female nudes who bulge with muscles and tendons, like anatomical diagrams. Thomas Rowlandson (1756–1827), on the other hand, did paint naked men and women (buxom and red-cheeked at both ends) but as these people are usually engaged in copulation Rowlandson's drawings were rated as pornography and thus enjoyed a very limited circulation.

The arbiter of British taste, the Royal Academy, was selective in the works which it showed on its walls. It was also restricted in space, and when it began to collapse because of the building work on the new Reform Club next door, it moved a few doors away, and a few years later to new premises on the site of the King's Mews, Charing Cross. The architect was William Wilkins who had recently made his name with his designs for University College, London, and the building was shared with what was to become the nucleus of the national collection. It is now the National Gallery, and the centre cupola, known as the 'pepper-pot', was the Life School, where models posed in the nude for students. The Royal Academy was not merely a place where pictures were hung for the edification of visitors, but a college of instruction.

The founding of the Royal Academy owes almost everything to the patronage and active help of King George III, who undertook to pay from his privy purse any deficit between the receipts derived from exhibitions and the expenditure incurred in the schools and on charitable bequests to suffering artists. From 1781 the Royal Academy was in profit, and no further calls have ever been made on the royal purse.

The Royal Academy retained its portion of the National Gallery until 1867, when it moved to its present site, at Burlington House, which was greatly enlarged over the years. Originally there were thirty-six Academicians, named by George III. The government of the Academy was by an 'Instrument', vested in a President and eight other persons who constituted a council. The Instrument fixed the number of Academicians at forty; in addition, there were twenty Associates, but this restriction was lifted in 1866. In theory there was then no limit to the number of Associates who could be elected and Academicians and Associates decided themselves who would join them. It was a tight and slightly self-satisfied clique, with strong views on what constituted art.

Rather surprisingly, with an internal ballot determining the exact constitution of the Royal Academy, the Academicians were not at any time a bunch of mediocrities. In other royal colleges, such as that of music, the principal was often merely a figurehead, at best an administrator and at worst a nuisance, but this was not true of the Royal Academy. Conversely, the men who ran the place—the keeper, the secretary, the treasurer and the librarian—were of little importance. In 1836, the year before Victoria came to the throne, the keeper was paid only £160 a year, and the secretary £140. To give this figure some reality, the average wage for a carpenter or plumber was £75 a year. (In 1863, the secretary was the better paid, at £400 a year.)

Soft focus adds to the charm.

Interestingly, light concentrates attention on the mirror.

Over-printing of the tree at right creates dimension.

Drama, in classical style.

It is interesting to compare these decorous nude
photographs with the nude paintings of the early- and mid-
Victorian artists; salaciousness is equally well avoided and
the same coyness is apparent.

Phaedria by William Edward Frost (1810–77), elected
Associate of the Royal Academy in 1846, and Academician
in 1870. On the reverse of the picture is inscribed an extract
from Spenser's *Faerie Queen*: 'Upon the bank they sitting did
espy, A daintie damsel dressing of her heare.' (There is no
mention in Spenser of the damsel being naked.)

The person who gave the Academy the lead was the President, and in the 130
years between the founding of the Academy and the end of the nineteenth century
there were only eleven Presidents, most of whom were certainly not nonentities and
several of whom were first-rate painters. These included two of the men who were
to establish the classical nude as a sacrosanct and—more important to the prudish
Victorian middle classes—a respectable subject, namely Lord Leighton and Sir
Edward Poynter.

3
ETTY,
THE
DEDICATED PAINTER

Royal Academicians in the late eighteenth and early nineteenth centuries were not bothered by questions of propriety and brushed off accusations of suggestiveness with impatience. The drawing and painting of the nude was to the artist commonplace, a test of ability, arousing no feelings of embarrassment or shame. Studies for the figures in the vast historical canvases so popular early in the nineteenth century were often made from nude models, as it was considered important to get the stance of the body right before any attempt was made to paint clothing or drapery. The nude sketch was an intermediate step in the execution of what were termed 'grand machines'.

Painters were also well aware of the heritage of the past, many of them having visited Italy and seen the great paintings of Raphael and Titian, and they were familiar with those which they had not actually seen, through engravings. The Academicians were well able to paint nudes, but there did not seem a market for them; they supplied what the customer wanted, and were well paid for doing so.

There was one exception: William Etty, born in York in 1787, the seventh son of a miller and baker famed for gingerbread. Artistic ability showed early, his first equipment being a farthing's worth of white chalk. He was apprenticed to a Hull printer and served seven years diligently from the age of eleven. At eighteen his uncle in London sent for him, and he studied art, drawing from the antique at a plaster-cast shop in Cock Lane, Smithfield.

On the strength of a picture on the theme of Psyche and Cupid, Etty approached the painter John Opie, a skilled producer of historical and religious pictures, and Opie and the artist Fuseli secured the young man's entrance to the Royal Academy School. A hundred guineas paid by his uncle brought him lodging and a modicum of tuition in the Greek Street home of Thomas Lawrence (1769–1830). Lawrence held the quaint post of limner (painter) to the King, for which he was knighted in 1815, and was to be President of the Royal Academy in the period 1820–30. He was too busy to lavish his time on young Etty who was instead asked to copy his works—flattering and glittering portraits of the rich and noble.

Etty left Lawrence after a year, finding solace and inspiration in the Life School at the Royal Academy, but it was not until 1811 that he succeeded in getting any pictures exhibited. This was at the British Institution, opened in 1806 for the 'Encouragement of Works of Dignity and Importance in Art' and endeavouring to foster modern art (for even then the Royal Academy was being branded as old-fashioned and out of tune with the new century). *The Times* gave their backing to the British Institution, and ignored the Royal Academy, and there were frequent complaints of the Academy's inadequate arrangements, its dinginess and its dirtiness.

The enthusiasm for the British Institution gradually wore off when it became apparent that the exhibitors there were no less of a clique than the Academicians. In the same year, Etty managed to get the Royal Academy to take another picture, a lavish historical work called *Telemachus Rescues the Princess Antiope from the Fury of the Wild Boar*.

Over the years he continued to exhibit, but to his associates he was a 'worthy plodding person, with no chance of ever becoming a good painter', and it was considered that his constant attendance at the Life School was decidedly unhealthy, and that he was becoming obsessed with naked women (as indeed was probably the

A preliminary sketch by William Etty, before he had refined
and brought to ripe perfection this trio of nudes in oil paint.
Etty's sketches often have more animation than his finished
paintings.

case). His brother Walter paid for William to visit Italy, and on his return Etty's paintings showed greater confidence, with *Pandora* exhibited at the British Institution in 1820 and *The Coral Finders* at the Royal Academy. When *Cleopatra* was shown in 1821 it made a great impression: Etty had arrived, and he was being referred to as 'the English Titian'.

In 1822 he paid another visit to Italy, sketching and copying. He was now in his mid-thirties, slovenly looking, with a head too large for his body and ungainly hands. Smallpox had scarred his face, and his long sandy hair was unkempt. High-minded and sober, with a strong sense of duty, he had no violent passions or vices, or so it appeared, except his preoccupation with painting nude women. With clothed women he was shy but impulsive, falling in and out of love, and making awkward advances which were always repulsed. Of one of the women he wrote:

> No one knows what anxiety and anguish I have borne. I fear I may have erred against propriety, even delicacy. Yet I know not.

When in doubt he asked advice of his brother Walter, who also relieved him of any financial worries, though these seemed to be in the process of ending when in 1824 Etty was elected an Associate of the Royal Academy. The following year he exhibited one of his largest and grandest works, *The Combat*, 10ft 4in by 13ft 3in, in which a half-naked woman attempts to intercede between two half-naked warring men, a fine picture full of movement which to many seemed to recapture the glories of the great days of Italian painting. The size frightened prospective buyers off, but it was bought by the artist John Martin, in a moment of enthusiasm, for £300. John Martin, whose sweeping luridly lit panoramas now receive the appreciation a long time denied to them, later regretted this purchase, but *The Combat* impressed Lord Darnley sufficiently for him to commission a painting of *The Judgement of Paris*.

Between 1825 and 1830 Etty painted three more large canvases, and in 1831 two of them, plus *The Combat*, were purchased by the Royal Scottish Academy and later transferred to the Scottish National Gallery where they held prime wall space well into the twentieth century, before being demoted to the basement. If nothing else, this enterprise on the part of the sober Scots proved that they saw nothing in these vast tableaux of sensual and writhing nudes to frighten off their countrymen, and this view was shared by the Royal Academicians, who nominated Etty as a full Academician in 1828, despite the gradually mounting accusations of indecency.

The Times, which had reluctantly conceded that the Royal Academy was there to stay even when ignoring its existence, was a leader in the campaign against Etty. His paintings were 'entirely too luscious for the public eye'. 'I have been accused of being a shocking and immoral man,' complained Etty, perplexed by the furore. 'Though bruised, I trust I am not broken. I hear a consciousness of something bidding me not to despair of doing that which after ages shall not let die.'

In 1824 he had left his old house in Stangate Walk, Lambeth, and moved to new premises at 14, Buckingham Street, Strand, where for the last twenty-five years of his life his niece kept house for him. Every day he would go to the Life School of the Royal Academy, rubbing shoulders with the students and enraging fellow Academicians who thought it demeaning for Etty to mingle with the learners. But this was Etty's life, ever striving to perfect his technique.

Although criticized on moral grounds, there were few artists who denied that in the painting of flesh Etty had no equals. He managed to produce a radiant glow, and it was said that he employed a 'secret medium'. When taxed with this he replied that the only medium he used was brains. At work he was quiet and diligent, sometimes taking off a glaze (a transparent colour wash over an existing layer of paint) with his thumb, at other times dabbing the surface with his pocket handkerchief or employing his finger nails, palette knife or indeed any object that was handy, to get

A fine oil sketch by Etty. His critics were often affronted by
the fact that Etty's models were so evidently Victorian
young ladies—the hair style here is unmistakable.

Wide-hipped and busty, the woman in this Etty sketch had
the qualities the mid-Victorian man liked. To earlier
painters, a nude seen from the back symbolized lust, but
hardly in this instance.

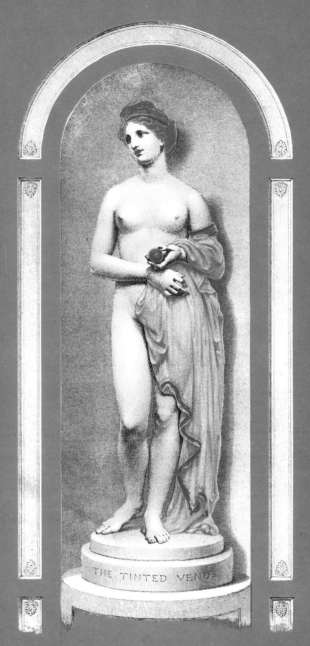

One of Lord Leighton's most celebrated paintings, *The Bath of Psyche*, exhibited at the Royal Academy in 1890, bought for the Chantrey Bequest and now to be seen at Leighton House (open to the public) on loan from the Tate Gallery.

The Tinted Venus by John Gibson, the most famous nude statue of the time, coloured with tinted wax and causing a sensation when it was first displayed. This engraving appeared in the pages of the *Art Journal*, the main art magazine of its day, and, although the engraver took some liberties, it is very like the genuine article.

Idyll by Lord Leighton, painted in 1880–1 and exhibited at the Royal Academy in 1881. The figure on the right was modelled on Lillie Langtry. The landscape beyond the figures is certainly one of the best to be found in Leighton's work.

the effect he wanted. To intensify the pearly glow he used tiny flecks of black and white judiciously placed. He was the supreme master of his art, though critics complained of his lack of finish, influenced by the careful detail and immaculate surfaces of many of the historical paintings so much in vogue.

In 1835 *The Observer* launched itself in an attack on Etty's paintings, maintaining that 'the Lord Mayor himself deserves at once to be sent to the treadmill for imprisoning a little Italian boy for hawking about the streets a naked Cupid, if such lascivious scenes are to be allowed at the Royal Academy with impunity'. We are not yet into the Victorian period, but the chasm between what was allowed outside the Royal Academy and what was allowed inside was already wide. The most innocuous of prints, if they depicted a naked woman, could result in the print-seller being hauled off to prison. The powers of those determined to maintain a high moral tone—especially for the benefit of others—were considerable; middle-class morality, often mistakenly believed to be a product of Victorian repression, was all too obviously a force to be reckoned with. The key to prurient thinking is that the viewer is affected by what he or, more generally she, sees, and considers this dangerous, not to themselves, but to those younger or lower in the social scale. In this context, lascivious was a handy word to describe not the picture itself but the effect that it might have on those others unfortunately lacking the critic's objectivity and self-restraint.

Naturally, many of these self-appointed censors were indignant that the recent interest in Greek sculpture should have made available to the general public the spectacle of nude bodies, but marble or any stone added an element of distance, of frigidity, to a nude statue. In addition, the Greeks were remote in time and the expressions on the statues' faces impersonal.

Even Etty's friends and supporters could not maintain that the nudes in his paintings were remote; they were clearly nineteenth-century English girls, idealized and generalized, but none the less contemporary. There are no fat women in Etty's paintings; they are all beautifully formed, whether depicted singly, as in *The Bather*, where the girl is up to her thighs in water diplomatically holding a towel, or in elaborate groupings, as in perhaps Etty's best-known painting, *Youth on the Prow and Pleasure at the Helm*, where the faces and the hair-styles are clearly those of the period in which it was painted. Its setting is ambiguous—a mythological never-never-land—but Etty did not feel that he was obliged to burden all his paintings with historical titles just to give him a defence against those who thought that he was painting merely dirty pictures.

That Etty painted modern women was a charge levelled at him time and time again. In 1843 *Blackwood's Magazine* criticized the Three Graces in the picture of that name for looking as though they had worn stays. It would have been surprising had they not. Half a century earlier the waist had been situated just beneath the breasts, but gradually it had dropped to its proper level and needed the constrictions of stays and corsets to keep it there. As late as 1886 the Pre-Raphaelite painter William Holman Hunt returned to the charge—'town models distorted by the modiste's art'. The paintings of William Etty still had the power to disturb.

There were other painters of the nude among Etty's contemporaries, and one of these was the high-minded and studious painter William Hilton (1786–1839). Many considered his Europa, in a painting where she is raped by a bull, too sexually

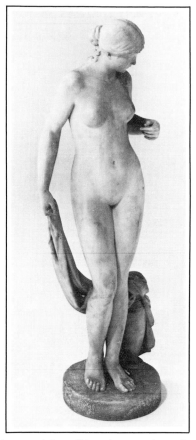

This sculpture might well be taken as a three-dimensional version of an Etty female nude. Actually it is a mid-nineteenth-century Italian sculpture and illustrates the universality of the type of woman Etty delighted to paint.

desirable. This mythological subject, rather perverted perhaps to modern thought, had been tackled by the masters of the past and was thus respectable, but Hilton went too far in persuading the viewer to identify with the bull. No painter however was as single-minded as Etty, inflexible in his pursuit of his goal, or obsession. During the last ten years of his life he struggled against asthma and rheumatism, but every day in all weather he would go down the hundred steps from his studio to the street and the Life School.

Only towards the end of his life was Etty getting large prices for his work, and throughout most of his life he was subsidized by his brother Walter. Membership of the Royal Academy had not brought William a fortune and at one time, even when he was famous, he owed Walter £4,000. He was not a businessman; he was surprised when a set of three pictures sold for £2,500 and again when it was said at Christie's that 'Etty sells for more than Raphael'.

As a young man he had been depressed by criticism, but in later life he strenuously defended himself:

Ladies' Combinations.
DELIGHTFULLY COMFORTABLE.
A REAL LUXURY IN UNDERWEAR.

THE DEEANJAY" COMBINATION

Criticism was sometimes levelled against Etty because it was
clear that his models had worn stays. Whether this was true
or not, the typical Etty nude shows no sign of the
constrictions of stays, corsets, or the kind of body-shaper
illustrated in this 1899 advertisement.

Finding God's most glorious work to be woman, I resolved to dedicate myself to painting, not the draper's or milliner's model, but God's more glorious work, more finely than had ever been done before.

He died in 1849. The importance of Etty in the history of the nude in Victorian art is impossible to overemphasize. That his works were bought by both private persons and national collections proves that there was a demand for the kind of painting of which he was the most accomplished exponent. It is true that he rarely received more than £300 a picture during his most fertile period, but in terms of today's values this would be in the region of £6,000. To affronted visitors to the Royal Academy and the British Institution it seemed as though Etty was churning out his nudes just for the purpose of enraging them, and after he had gone there was a backlash against them, and all that they stood for. Etty represented a tradition which had no place in the latter half of the nineteenth century.

4
THE NUDE
IN SCULPTURE

It is curious that the suspicion and sometimes downright distaste with which painters of the nude were greeted in the years leading up to the reign of Queen Victoria was not directed at sculptors as well. One of the reasons for this was that nude statuary had been about in such large quantities for many years that unless it was indecent it was accepted.

The most popular of pre-Victorian sculptors was an Italian who spearheaded the classical revival, and whose name was known to everyone with some pretensions to taste—Antonio Canova (1757–1822). He had looked at all the statuary of the past—Greek, Roman, Renaissance, and Baroque—and decided that he could go one better and invest his own sculpture with pathos and more popular appeal. The *British Cyclopaedia* of 1834 complained that:

> . . . an opera-stage taint infects all his earlier works . . . even in the statue of *The Kneeling Magdalen* there is enough of affectation to poison the loveliest, the most exquisite, workmanship and the most finished charms of shape.

Of his *Dancers*, '. . . no damsels of the ballet ever leaped so high, or exposed their charms so lavishly'.

Although the *British Cyclopaedia* did not put it so succinctly, Canova's female nudes were saucy, and it is not surprising that the French sculptors were heavily influenced by him and his contemporaries. French statuary was a three-dimensional version of the kind of painting practised by Boucher, and the sculptors did all they could to make marble sensuous, both in the public and private domain. Many sculptors did not feel that they need alter their style for outdoor statuary, and people were affronted by the group of nude dancers outside the Paris Opera House, the work of Carpeaux in 1869.

The large quantity of nude statues is understandable when we consider the options open to a sculptor. In painting, there are certain classes where nudes are necessarily omitted—portrait, landscapes, and marine. The most important branch of sculpture is statuary; there are two kinds of statuary, the clothed and the unclothed. Marble does not lend itself too readily to the imitation of clothes, though the immense skill of many sculptors frequently makes us overlook this. The Italians in particular were very proud of their abilities to reproduce anything in marble, their speciality being the veil. (One of the big draws of the Great Exhibition of 1851 were the veiled statues by an obscure Italian sculptor named Monti, statues which were endlessly copied especially in Parian, a type of porcelain invented to imitate marble.)

On the other hand, marble was the ideal material to simulate flesh. Though in sculpting the nude the artist was faced with fewer technical problems, he could make his figures appear ridiculous by representing a person obviously in the habit of wearing clothes, a very different thing from the purity of the ancient Greek treatment of the nude. This was especially true in male statues intended for the public domain, whether in marble, imitation marble such as coade stone (patented and marketed by Mrs Eleanor Coade from her manufactory in Lambeth) or bronze.

The Napoleonic Wars gave an impetus to British sculpture. There were so many men to commemorate, and so many towns and cities anxious to supplement local pride with a statue. In addition, the new rich middle classes found that statuary in

Throughout much of Victorian painting and
sculpture there lurks a curious sado-
masochistic element, typified in the theme of
Andromeda by Bell, shown here, exhibited in
the Great Exhibition of 1851. 'The figure is
very elegantly conceived', said the catalogue,
'and has a charming simplicity of treatment.'

the drawing-room was more acceptable to their taste, and more of a talking point, than the 'black masters' of the past, and comparable with giant historical paintings. There was a mania for sculpture of all kinds.

Stated the *British Cyclopaedia*:

> The public monuments scattered about our squares and principal streets are generally of bronze, and many of these metal kings, warriors, and statesmen, grim with dust and smoke, look at a distance like so many black shapeless masses without form or character.

When examined closely, these bronzes could surprise the observant, and this was delicately hinted when the sculptor Westmacott (1775–1856) was praised. He had 'obeyed the admonition of our cold climate, and respected the blushes of our ladies, and clothed some of his works in the costume of the country'.

Many of the most provocative of monumental nudes were found in cathedrals and churches to commemorate the fallen or the dead. In 1802 the naval captain Burgess was honoured in St Paul's Cathedral by the sculptor Thomas Banks, and was naked except for drapery falling down his torso and concealing his private parts by an inch or so. Originally the drapery was even less concealing, but it was lengthened after religious protest. Also in St Paul's is the monument to Sir William Ponsonby, killed at Waterloo when his horse stumbled, and carved by William Theed and Edward Baily. He is not quite so revealing as Captain Burgess, but he is wearing what seems to be the same piece of drapery.

The partiality for depicting men of action nearly nude, however inappropriate, was shared by Henry Rossi, whose figure *The Batsman* is facing up to the bowler wearing two items only, a kerchief around the neck and what seems to be a truss (known in cricket today as 'the box'). This became an immensely popular statuette, and spin-offs from marbles were cheap—plaster-casts were sold for two guineas, and Italians used these to mould replicas at half a crown apiece. Marble substitute was also inexpensive, whether it was coade stone or lithargelite, a moulded substance marketed by Mr Bubb from his depot in Grafton Street, London. Bubb was not only an entrepreneur but a sculptor, and he executed more than fifty statues for Regent's Park.

One of the most famous pieces of sculpture of pre-Victorian England was *Eve*, the work of Edward Baily (1788–1867), the co-sculptor of the Sir William Ponsonby monument, which was 'loveliness personified, and though undraped, yet breathes the purest spirit of chastity. Simple description indeed can hardly do justice to the peculiar beauty, simplicity, and modesty of this figure.' Baily was to survive well into the mid-Victorian period, and diversify into obelisks when the age for filling the towns and cities of Great Britain with naked statues had gone.

The proliferation of these statues was often noted with amusement by overseas visitors, one of whom was the American novelist Nathaniel Hawthorne, who on a visit to Britain in 1856 wished 'it would not so generally happen that English warriors go into battle almost nude'. The day after this entry in his note-book he went to the British Museum, and made his pronouncement on that establishment:

This life-size sculpture by Professor Kiss of Berlin, *The Amazon*, was sufficiently famous to be parodied in the pages of *Punch*. It was exhibited in the Great Exhibition of 1851. The sculptor used zinc, one eighth of the cost of bronze. These zinc sculptures were 'admirably calculated for gardens in England'.

It quite crushes a person to see so much at once, and I wandered from hall to hall with a weary and heavy heart, wishing (Heaven forgive me!) that the Elgin Marbles and the frieze of the Parthenon were all burnt into lime.

Without the Elgin Marbles and the enthusiasm generated by them, he would not have been subject to the sight of so many naked warriors.

Contorted as are many of the poses of the fallen dead, giving the sculptor scope to display his skill, no one could say that the heroes of the Napoleonic Wars immortalized in bronze or stone were erotic. This would have been a gigantic lapse of taste. However, the task of making a memorial to a dead woman erotic did not daunt M. C. Wyatt (1777–1862).

Princess Charlotte was the only daughter of the future George IV and Caroline of Brunswick. A lively tempestuous girl, she was brought up in strict seclusion, seeing her father at odd intervals and her mother, the estranged Caroline, for two hours a week. An engagement to Prince William of Orange was broken off after six months, to her father's anger, and instead she married Prince Leopold of Saxe-Coburg. She died in childbirth in 1817, aged twenty-one, distressing a nation.

Wyatt loved the grand gesture, and his memorial to Princess Charlotte in St George's chapel, Windsor, taxed his ingenuity to the full. There was a fashion for pictures depicting dead children being wafted up to heaven by angels, and Wyatt decided to do the same sort of thing in three dimensions, with a before and after time sequence. The princess is moving heavenwards, thinly draped with one breast exposed, inoffensive to those accustomed to religious pictures, but beneath the main tableau of the princess and two angels—one of them holding the dead infant—the naked body of the princess is lying on an oblong tomb, the carved draperies almost indecently moulded to her body. To complete the effect, the fingers of one hand droop from beneath the falling drapery.

This startling monument was put in place in 1824, paid for by shilling subscriptions from the public, and it is significant in that it established a decided liaison between death and sex. This was also sometimes explored to a macabre extent by French nineteenth-century artists until their work becomes almost necrophilic. The memorial to Princess Charlotte led to a profusion of provocative funeral monuments in the great cemeteries of London. (Kensal Green was consecrated in 1832, Highgate in 1839.)

Sculptors enjoyed prestige and considerable wealth, and many lived to a great age. One of the most controversial was John Gibson (1790–1866), the son of a Welsh market gardener, who always carried three packages around with him, for the reason that the Greeks liked the quantity three. As a young man in search of anatomical knowledge he went grave-robbing with fellow artists. They came across 'a very beautiful girl about sixteen; her face was full and round. How sweet and innocent she looked in death!'

As a boy Gibson was apprenticed to a cabinet-maker and later to a wood-carver, but he was taken up by the proprietor of a marble works, who passed off Gibson's juvenile but accomplished work as his own. Gibson went to Rome in 1817, and spent much of his life in Italy, studying under Canova through whom he obtained many commissions. He studied casts of the Elgin Marbles in Rome, and determined that all his sculpture would demonstrate purity of character and beauty of form. He took many of his models from the streets of Rome, and became a specialist in carved Cupids, whom he called 'the little god of soft tribulations'. Roman children were accustomed to walk about almost naked, providing a never-ending stream of models.

There are strong parallels with the painter Etty. Both were devoted to their art, both were repressed and sought fulfilment in the exposition of the nude, and both were fired and stimulated by what they saw in Italy. Gibson was far more versatile, renowned for his portrait figures and busts, including a Queen Victoria supported by Justice and Clemency in the Houses of Parliament. (In 1957 Justice and Clemency were taken away, leaving only the Queen.) In 1833 he was elected an

Eagle and Child by the French sculptor, Le Chesne, was, declared the 1851 Exhibition catalogue, 'a powerfully told story, but of too painful a kind'. The theme of the nude woman under threat was a constant one among Victorian painters and sculptors.

Associate of the Royal Academy, in 1836 a Royal Academician, and he was strongly represented in the Great Exhibition of 1851, in which nudes proliferated—in porcelain, adorning clock sets, decorating vases or plaques, holding up candlesticks, forming the handles of urns and cutlery, and even protruding from the ends of curtain-rods. Although intended as a display of 'Works of Art and Industry' from 'All the Nations of the World' the Great Exhibition was, in its way, a celebration of the nude. The massive illustrated catalogue set out to show engravings of 'the most interesting and the most suggestive of the various objects exhibited', and, indeed, the clergy interpreted the word suggestive in their own collective way. Bishops refused to attend the opening ceremony unless the many nude statues were decently clothed.

There was no attempt on the part of the sculptors to censor their nudes. Some of the figures have skimpy drapery, but many are totally naked. In the catalogue of the Great Exhibition the private parts of the men were invariably covered either with a fig-leaf or, more usually, a shell-like object—the compiler of the catalogue had already seen the dangers and had indulged in his own censorship. But for a sub-

A fountain incorporating nude figures shown in the Paris
Universal Exhibition of 1867. Since antiquity, nude figures,
mainly male, were used in fountain design and many were
furnished with tails. The mermaid theme was very popular
throughout the second half of the nineteenth century.

sequent event, the catalogue could have been accepted as a realistic account of
objects as they were.

In 1854 thirteen eminent people wrote to the Directors of the Crystal Palace
complaining that the statues of nude males intended for permanent display, being
accurate in detail, would in 'exhibition to promiscuous crowds of men and women
prove very destructive to that natural modesty which is one of the outworks of
virtue, and which a great French writer has called "one of the barriers which Nature
herself has placed in the way of crime"'. In other words, men with penises and
testicles, whether in stone or not, were a perpetual threat to the stability of the
nation. The Directors of the Crystal Palace yielded to the pressure, and ordered
emasculation by hammer and chisel. Home and beauty were saved.

With the Great Exhibition of 1851 we are fourteen years into the reign of Queen
Victoria, with hardly a hint, except from the clergy, of the decades of suppression
which lay ahead. More remarkable still we see the elements of sadism and
masochism which were to form a staple part of the underground empire of
pornography.

Nude statues with sado-masochistic overtones were not
merely a British and French phenomenon, but a European
one. *The Captive Mother* was executed by the Danish sculptor
Stephan Sinding in 1889.

Using, as a front, scenes from mythology, there was a clear delight in depicting naked women tied up or otherwise 'in bondage'. One of the best known of this fashionable class was *Andromeda* by John Bell, cast in bronze by the Coalbrook Dale Company. 'The figure', declared the catalogue of the exhibition, 'is very elegantly conceived, and has a charming simplicity of treatment.' A wide-hipped big-breasted Victorian beauty stands somewhat embarrassedly on what looks like an ornate fountain, a thin chain wound round her upper thigh and leading between her legs to the base.

Quite as ambiguous was a group by the French sculptor Le Chesne, called *Eagle and Child*, in which a voluptuous naked woman, arms outstretched, is attacked by an eagle, while her child, whose face expresses curiosity rather than terror, rises up beside her. The sculptor promised to continue the story with a tableau in which the woman strangles the eagle and saves the child. There were a number of exhibits in which naked or partly naked women were attacked by wild beasts, and typical of these was *Amazon Attacked by a Tiger*, the work of Professor Kiss of Berlin. Except for a curious type of cap, similar to those worn by Republicans in the French Revolution, the Amazon is clearly a German *fräulein*, built on the same lines as John Bell's *Andromeda*, and not so popular as the chained girl for she is clearly winning. Many of these sculptures were being cast in zinc by Geiss of Berlin. Zinc was one-eighth the cost of bronze, and such figures were being marketed for display in English gardens.

Artemis by William Hamo Thornycroft (1850–1925) was
exhibited at the Royal Academy in 1880. He later sculpted a
statue of General Gordon for Trafalgar Square, followed by
a variety of other notables, for which he was knighted in
1917. *Artemis* was his first major success.

Perhaps the most popular of these damsels in distress was *The Greek Slave*, carved in Rome in 1843 by the American sculptor, Hiram Powers (1805–73). As a young man, Powers was a reading-room attendant, a clerk in a general store, and a mechanic in a clock and organ factory, before trying his hand at sculpture. The enthusiasm with which his work was greeted in Washington encouraged him to go to Italy in 1837, where he remained for the rest of his life. He lived on commissions for busts but reserved his talent for nudes such as *Eve* and *The Greek Slave*—which was reproduced in many forms and made the nude statue acceptable in America, where the attitude towards the naked figure closely paralleled that in Britain.

The massed ranks of statuary in the Great Exhibition may have been daunting, but in the absence of painting, unrepresented in the Exhibition except for those carried out in novel materials, they showed that art could have a public appeal previously thought unbelievable. In one day in October 1851 more than a hundred thousand visitors crowded into the Crystal Palace to gawp at the exhibits and perhaps snigger at the nudes. In a fit of enthusiasm the Corporation of London voted to fill the Egyptian Hall in the Mansion House with statues, including the luscious *Lea* by Patrick MacDowell based on the Medici *Venus*, at a total cost of £10,000.

It seemed that the nude statue had reached perfection, chained or unchained, male or female, sporting drapery or a fig-leaf, but there was one further development to come, and this was *The Tinted Venus*, by John Gibson, shown at the Exhibition of 1862 and carved a few years earlier. Gibson maintained that the Greek statues had originally been coloured, and he applied coloured wax to the surface of his quite decorous Venus. She was more of a 'grisette than goddess', complained the poet Elizabeth Barrett Browning, and many found the statue offensive. Marble in its native state was cold and aloof, but by tinting it there was too great a resemblance to real flesh for comfort. However, Gibson's innovation was not followed, and when *The Tinted Venus* was sold at Sotheby's Belgravia in the 1960s it was still possible to see why, a hundred years earlier, it had had the power to disturb.

5
THE EARLY
VICTORIAN ART SCENE

In 1837 Queen Victoria came to the throne, and few monarchs have echoed so closely the thoughts and aspirations of their subjects. As a girl she had been taught drawing, and her little sketches of what she saw around her are expressive and accomplished. She liked artists to portray what she herself saw, and the adventurous landscapes of Turner she considered 'most extraordinary', meaning that she did not particularly like them, could not fully understand what the man was driving at, and was unlikely to commission any work from him (unlike other members of the aristocracy and nobility who did). Her preferences were for painters such as Landseer (1802–73), who portrayed dogs with human expressions and stags at bay.

If there was a fault to find with Landseer it was that there was insufficient finish, and this opinion was shared with Prince Albert, whom she married in 1840. A portrait was valued in so far as it resembled the sitter, or if possible showed the sitter in a favourable light. If the colour was wrong, she told the artist so. She was not concerned that colour was affected by moonlight, sunlight, or candlelight. The Queen and Prince Albert were supremely confident that their judgement on art matters was infallible; at Windsor the Rembrandts and the Van Dycks were put high on the walls so that the family portraits, especially those by their particular favourite, the German Winterhalter (1805-73), could be better displayed.

Prince Albert proclaimed that as a young man he had studied oil painting, lithography, and engraving, not with a view to practising the arts but as a prelude to giving advice about them. The Prince was especially interested in systems and an overall design, and when he interfered in the arts he was listened to at first with indifference but later with attention as it became apparent that he was a man who worked hard at being Prince Consort and that there was considerable Teutonic sense in what he said. When he decided that it would be a good idea if the national collection, which was set out higgledy-piggledy in the National Gallery, should be grouped into German Schools, Italian Schools and Dutch Schools for the convenience of not only the staff but also the public, his plan was enthusiastically adopted.

It was Prince Albert's enthusiasm and gift for organization which led to the Great Exhibition of 1851, where the supremacy of the British in all things was hammered home to foreigners of every cast. He was also the prime mover in the Art Treasures Exhibition at Manchester in 1857, seen by more than a million people. For the first time in generations the masterpieces owned by the aristocracy, usually hung on ill-lit walls or stored by the dozen in basements and cellars, were wheeled out—often to the regret of their owners, for they were, at the close of the exhibition, wheeled back with their credentials dashed. Far too often the 'black masters' labelled with prestigious names turned out to be arrant fakes or third-rate hack work.

Opposite The Baths of Caracalla by Laurence Alma-Tadema, one of his grandest pictures, showing not only his command over the nude figure but his complete mastery of architectural detail. Alma-Tadema delighted in intimate detail, and his women are far less formidable than the statuesque creations of his contemporaries.

That a monarch, even the husband of a monarch, should want to act as a cultural overlord was sufficiently novel for Prince Albert to be regarded with interest. In 1851 he appeared at the Royal Academy dinner, in order to accept the Academicians' thanks for the work he had done in promoting the Great Exhibition; in response he praised the current President, Sir Charles Eastlake, known now mainly on account of his writings on art and not for his lurid pictures of Italian bandits and sanctimonious Christian subjects. To the Prince, Eastlake's main justifications for holding his post was his 'kindness of heart and refinement of feeling', and in Albert's speech there was great stress not on the artist's technique but on 'warmth of feeling'.

He was strenuously against criticism of artists. 'An unkind word of criticism passes like a cold blast over their tender shoots, and shrivels them up.' He went on to modern art:

> In this respect our times are peculiarly unfavourable when compared with those when Madonnas were painted in the seclusion of convents; for we have now, on the one hand, the eager competition of a vast array of artists of every degree of talent and skill, and, on the other, as judge, a great public, for the greater part wholly uneducated in art, and thus led by professional writers, who often strive to impress the public with a great idea of their own artistic knowledge by the merciless manner in which they treat works which cost those who produced them the highest efforts of mind or feeling.

This, in the guise of an after-dinner speech, was in the nature of a manifesto, and it was taken to heart. It was a plea for the innocuous and all that would not offend the great British public, or make too great a demand on their intelligence. The artists who were doing their best to cater for the masses should not be attacked by critics, who might have their own ideas on what was good or bad in art.

Culture for all was advocated not only by Prince Albert but by many others as well. If the working classes could be diverted from their usual leisure pursuits of drinking and womanizing then they would become a satisfactory section of society, taking their place in the order of things. If they persisted with their self-improvement it was logical that they would become happier and more content. There would also be less danger of them rising. Fear of civil war was always present during the nineteenth century, and there was always a danger that what had happened in France could happen in Britain.

One of the instruments of improvement was the Museums Act of 1845. This gave permission for local authorities to levy a small rate to pay for the erection and the running of museums and art galleries. Many authorities used this money to

Opposite A Favourite Custom by Lawrence Alma-Tadema, in which the technical problem of painting a figure in water was beautifully solved. Alma-Tadema always took care to ensure that his naked women were in a situation where nakedness was appropriate, as in baths.

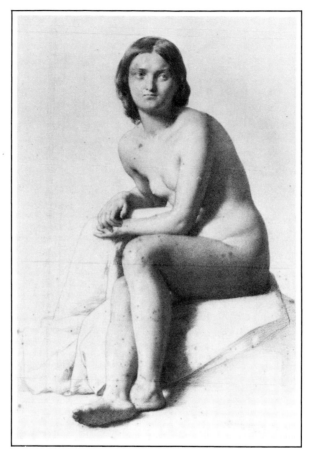

William Mulready (1786–1863) was best known for his
scenes of everyday life and book illustrations, but this
splendid life study, made at the Kensington School in 1862,
shortly before he died, shows his mastery of the nude.

build vast edifices to reflect the glory of their towns and cities, and were not too
concerned with what went inside them. They only had to look at the British
Museum, which was dusty, neglected, with the exhibits badly arranged, and often
piled in heaps because the curator and experts were uncertain what they were, and
were otherwise engaged.

On the other hand, some administrators of provincial art galleries and museums
were enlightened, and bought works by modern artists. They often persuaded rich
collectors to lend them pictures. There is every evidence that the working classes
did find pleasure in visiting art galleries and museums, if only for the reason that
they were free. They also enjoyed looking at cycloramas, panoramas, osmoramas
and dioramas, educational canvases, tableaux or models representing earthquakes,
natural disasters or historical and geographical scenes, often accompanied by mood
music and clever lighting effects.

The enthusiasm that followed the popular success of the Great Exhibition

William Holman Hunt (1827–1910) was a founder-member
of the Pre-Raphaelites, and one would be hard put to it to
find a nude in any of his finished paintings. This study was
for *The Lady of Shalott*, and a wax model was made from it to
assist in the final (clothed) painting.

seemed to prove that the common people were well on their way to enlightenment. Of course there were still some who frequented art galleries just to snigger.

On 26 March 1856 the novelist Nathaniel Hawthorne visited the National Gallery:

There were a great many people in the gallery, almost entirely of the middle, with a few of the lower classes; and I should think that the effect of the exhibition must at least tend towards refinement. Nevertheless, the only emotion that I saw displayed was in broad grins on the faces of a man and two women at sight of a small picture of Venus, with a Satyr peeping at her with an expression of gross animal delight and merriment. Without being aware of it, this man and the two women were of that same Satyr breed.

In his address to the Academy, Prince Albert was opposed to the laws of the market in so far as they affected paintings:

William Edward Frost (1819–77) was strongly influenced by
Etty, and sustained himself by painting portraits, of which
he did more than three hundred. He was very fond of this
kind of grouping, assigning various titles. This painting is
called *The Muses*.

The works of art, by being publicly exhibited and offered for sale, are becoming articles of trade, following as such the unreasoning laws of markets and fashion; and public and even private patronage is swayed by their tyrannical influence.

It seemed as if he wished art to be in the hands of amateurs whose sole aim in life was to paint pleasing pictures. This cannot have pleased those Academicians who relied on the sales of their pictures to supply money to live on, and when he spoke of the times being peculiarly unfavourable to artists he was wide of the mark.

Paintings, to Prince Albert, were either a kind of wallpaper or a gratifying reminder of his good luck in marrying into the British Royal Family, but to others, who sustained British art, they were status symbols—and investments.

Artists who painted as the fancy took them had mixed fortunes. A painter such as Turner (1775–1851) was not appreciated by the masses nor by most of the critics, with the exception of John Ruskin and the perplexed but appreciative author of *Vanity Fair*, Thackeray. Critics usually favoured heavy sarcasm, which they thought was guaranteed to turn an artist to jelly. Of Turner's entries for the Royal Academy of 1842 the *Athenaeum* wrote: 'This gentleman has on former occasions chosen to paint with cream, or chocolate, yolk of egg or currant jelly,—here he uses his whole array of kitchen stuff.' Nothing had been seen like Turner, as Thackeray said, but this did not stop his work selling, even the experimental paintings of his later years. (He died in 1851, leaving £140,000 to found an asylum for distressed artists, a scheme thwarted by cunning lawyers.)

This has the same theme as the previous illustration but is
rather more finished and with additional background detail.
It is entitled *L'Allegro* and was reproduced in the *Art
Journal* in 1856, thus being given immediate respectability,
though after 1850 Frost's reputation was in decline.

A distressed artist whom he could have helped while he was still alive was
Benjamin Robert Haydon (1786–1846), who also painted what he wanted without
reference to current taste—huge historical paintings which had gone out of fashion.
In 1820 his *Christ's Entry into Jerusalem* had made £1,700 in gate money when
displayed in the Egyptian Hall, Piccadilly. (The Egyptian Hall had been opened in
1812 to house a natural history collection, and from 1819 was used for exhibitions
and concerts.)

In 1846 he once again rented space in the Egyptian Hall to display his two latest
gigantic canvases, inserting an advertisement in *The Times* urging 'every Briton
who has pluck in his bosom and a shilling in his pocket [to] crowd to his works
during the Easter week'. In the same building the dwarf 'General' Tom Thumb was
on display. Haydon watched the public stream past the door, and inserted another
advertisement in *The Times*:

Exquisite Feeling of the English People for High Art—
General Tom Thumb last week received 12,000 people, who paid him £600:
B. R. Haydon was honoured by the visits of 133½, producing £5 13s. 6d.,
being a reward for painting two of his finest works . . .

Hounded by creditors, reviled by critics who rarely found such a sitting duck as
Haydon, scorned by the Royal Academy with which he had conducted a persistent
and self-defeating feud, Haydon was granted £50 by Sir Robert Peel from a special

fund, but it was too late to save the artist from despair, and he killed himself, cutting his own throat and shooting himself in the head.

It was a lesson to fellow artists not to ignore supply and demand, with the implicit warning not to cross the Royal Academy. There was also another major lesson to be learned from the tragedy of Haydon—that no matter how grandiose a conception, this mattered nothing if the execution and technique were faulty—and Haydon was inclined to be slapdash when the excitement of painting was upon him—or not in tune with the kind of painting then popular.

The Royal Academy Exhibition of that year was little different from those of previous or succeeding seasons. The big picture at the exhibition was held to be *The Ordeal by Touch* by Daniel Maclise (1806–70). Maclise's paintings had everything the early Victorian liked—bright colour, pin-sharp detail and a commanding technique. He used literary themes, and his pictures based on scenes from Shakespeare were made famous by innumerable engravings. He moved in a circle which included Charles Dickens and two of the other Academy successes of 1846— William Mulready (1786–1863) who painted admirable scenes from everyday life and who stands up marvellously well today, and Edwin Landseer, whose immensely popular *Stag at Bay* told a story that could be grasped in two seconds.

Pictures which told a story could hardly fail to succeed with the public, and if the story came from literature so much the better. Shakespeare was always there to be browsed through, and Goldsmith's *Vicar of Wakefield* was being well thumbed to see what charming images it would yield. The pictures should point a moral, or at least make an appeal to serious minds. However, it is clear that the presence of two of Etty's nude paintings, with mythological titles to ricochet any critical bullets, did not make a literary story obligatory, while the six entries of Turner prove that there was no lack of enterprise in the Hanging Committee, the Academicians who selected the exhibits.

Thackeray summed up the 1846 Royal Academy Exhibition:

The English now paint from the *heart* more than of old. They do not aim at such great subjects as heretofore, or at subjects which the world is pleased to call great, viz., tales from Hume or Gibbon of royal personages under various circumstances of battle, murder, and sudden death . . . The heroic has been deposed; and our artists, in place, cultivate the pathetic and the familiar. . . . The younger painters are content to exercise their art on subjects far less exalted: a gentle sentiment, an agreeable, quiet incident, a tea-table tragedy, or a bread-and-butter idyll.

This is worth quoting at length because it seems the ideal recipe for insipidity, and that it was not says a good deal for the skills of the artists who managed to infuse life into the most wooden of subjects. The truth, of course, is that they would have made a decent job of any subject, if it had paid. They were consummate technicians, and this is what the buyer wanted. He could then look and marvel, wondering how the artist got this effect or that, and being uplifted by the strong moral tone.

They were pictures that could be set before wives and daughters without danger of the fair sex having the vapours, pictures which obviously took a long time to paint and, with the bonus of a famous signature, clearly cost a good deal of money. They indicated the status of the owner just as well as the horses in the stable, the quality of the carriage, the size of the house, and the number of the servants. The Victorians may have been decorous and prim, on the outside at least, but above all they were money conscious.

So we have a range of pictures guaranteed not to alarm, with Mulready having his characters choosing a wedding gown, C. R. Leslie showing us the reading of a will (a favourite ceremony in rich families where relatives often died unexpectedly), Charles Eastlake displaying his tender feelings with a picture about nuns, and W. P. Frith providing quiet humour on a theme from Molière.

How do nudes fit into this? There is only one answer. With the exception of Etty, regarded as a kind of licensed buffoon, they do not. Nudes were a tool of the trade, hired by the day or the week to go to the artists' studios and strike poses, to be sketched in pencil, charcoal, or colour wash before being decently presented, clothed, on the finished painting. Some artists did not need to employ models, but worked from memory or imagination, or they used lay figures—jointed models which could be adjusted to imitate most human postures.

A painterly and subdued picture by George Frederic Watts
(1817–1904), without the symbolism and careless finish that
often characterized Watts's work. It is called *Hero*. Hero is
waiting for her lover Leander, who every night swam the
Hellespont to visit her.

Shortly after his dissertation on the Royal Academy Exhibition of 1846 Thackeray made his opinions more overt, and attacked the insipidity of contemporary art, calling it 'the milk-and-water of human kindness', though making an exception of Landseer, whose occasional excursions into savagery echoed something in Thackeray (who was a complex character with, for example, a delight in watching public executions).

Many art-lovers who had not had the opportunity of visiting the Royal Academy were also depressed by the sickening sentimentality which they saw in the pictures when reproduced as engravings. This was hardly fair on the artists, for the engravers in wood and metal were often not of the first flight, and exaggerated features and attitudes, or, if the story demanded a modicum of attention, simplified the picture so that the message would get home in a new medium. Even Etty's paintings could become so desexualized when transmogrified into the new medium that they could pass as genteel illustrations for the fashionable drawing-room annuals.

Not surprisingly, many young men with the hope of becoming artists contrasted the even tenor of the art life in London with the energy and boisterousness of that abroad, compared the accomplished utterances of the English painters with the genius and gusto of Delacroix (1798–1863) in France and the fervent and sometimes frenzied zeal of the modern German school. Among these painters were those who were to establish the cult of the nude on the walls of the Royal Academy once and for all.

6
LEIGHTON, THE OLYMPIAN

Although it was standard practice for established artists to take in promising students, both in England and on the Continent, the English artists did it with a sense of condescension, particularly when they were—such as Sir Thomas Lawrence—gentlemen first and painters second. Foreign painters were often more enthusiastic and extrovert, not bothering much whether they had patrons or whether their work would sell on the open market, and glad to earn the guineas of English pupils.

Typical of the rising generation of artists, coming of age at the time of the Great Exhibition, was Frederic Leighton. His grandfather was court physician to the Tsar of Russia, and his father, learning Russian in six months, managed to pass medical examinations in Russia, practised there, and returned to England a rich man. Frederic was born in Scarborough in 1830, and the family moved to Bath, and thence to London, but the stay was not lengthy for Mrs Leighton was of a delicate disposition, and the family went to Europe, hoping that travel would help cure her.

Journeying in considerable style the Leightons went to Germany and Switzerland, wintering in Italy as was fashionable. Frederic picked up French, Italian, and German, becoming fluent in them, and his father, hoping that the boy would be a doctor, instructed him in anatomy, which proved valuable to the artist. Frederic wished to be an artist, and on the advice of Hiram Powers the sculptor, resident in Florence, Dr Leighton gave his approval, and Frederic was enrolled in the Florence Academy.

Competent as his instructors were, Frederic Leighton wanted something better, and in Frankfurt he became a pupil of Jacob von Steinle, a member of a group of artists called the Nazarenes, who sought inspiration in the religion of the Middle Ages, especially the more bleak and austere sector, which was reflected in their paintings. The Leightons set up base in Frankfurt from 1846 to 1852, but were always on the move. In 1848 Frederic had a studio in Brussels, where he met Belgian painters of an alien cast who executed exuberant and sometimes mad pictures. Antoine Wiertz's (1806–65) *The Suicide* was painted to deter young men from killing themselves, his *Thoughts and Visions of a Decapitated Head* was to lead hopefully to the abolition of the guillotine, and a painting depicting a clenched fist reaching out from a closed coffin was part of a campaign against premature burial—a popular topic of conversation in Europe where corpses in the mortuary had bells tied to their hands and feet to warn attendants that they were not yet ready to go.

It was a world away from the frigid propaganda of the Nazarenes, a universe away from the polite nothings of British academic art. Back in England for the Great Exhibition, the handsome and gifted Frederic was courted by the Royal Academicians and a great future was prophesied for him. But the time was not ripe for Leighton to show his mettle, and he settled in Rome, meeting the sculptor John Gibson, who did not care much for painting, and being introduced into fashionable society by Mrs Adelaide Sartoris, née Kemble, one of a great theatrical family. She became a proxy mother to him.

To the British and American contingent in Rome, Frederic Leighton seemed almost too good to be true, a linguist, high-spirited, the best waltzer in Rome, always willing to be called upon when a spare male was needed, yet at the same time working on a painting that would take the Royal Academy by storm. This was a massive picture, *Cimabue's Madonna Carried in Procession Through the Streets of Florence*,

A Leighton masterpiece, *Venus Disrobing for the Bath*, a picture which caused a great stir when it was exhibited in 1867 and shocked the clergy and the middle classes. Considering the climate of the time and the explicit eroticism of the picture this is hardly surprising.

a boring subject painted with immaculate thoroughness, exhibited at the Royal Academy in 1855, given a prominent place, and bought by Queen Victoria.

Ruskin described it as 'a very important and very beautiful' picture, and the word was immediately about that in Frederic Leighton Britain had an artist of top calibre and a man not without mystery, single, living abroad. He was now in Paris and not Italy or Germany; it was as though he had squeezed them dry. Friendly with the English artists in Paris, he was more interested in the grand life than in Bohemian scruffiness, and in making contact with artists such as Ary Scheffer, William Bouguereau, and Leon Gérôme, clever technicians with astonishing lapses of taste and a gift for the odd and the macabre.

Leighton's 1856 picture for the Royal Academy was *The Triumph of Music*, and he confidently expected to repeat his coup of the previous year. The critics eyed it, and noted that the key figure, Orpheus, was playing a violin. The violin, being a fairly modern instrument, was unlikely to be in existence for Orpheus to play, or so the critics claimed. As Orpheus was purely fictitious anyway Leighton could have maintained that the violin, being such a delightful instrument and so superior to the primitive lyre, was in use in the mythological world. He was, however, as his friend Mrs Elizabeth Barrett Browning reported, 'cut up unmercifully' by his picture's tepid reception, as he was by the lack of interest in his exhibit at the British Institution. This was a costume scene based on Shakespeare's *Romeo and Juliet* which, although sold, went for four hundred pounds instead of guineas. The twenty-pounds difference was trifling, but gentlemen-artists thought in terms of guineas.

Despite these minor upsets, Leighton was obviously destined for success and had already been tipped as a future President of the Royal Academy. He worked solidly away, perfecting his technique, trying his hand on religious pictures and doing some illustrative work for one of the lavish pictorial editions of the Bible then in vogue. He also illustrated George Eliot's novel *Romola* when it was serialized in the *Cornhill Magazine*, and when he went abroad, as he did frequently, he did evocative on-the-spot sketches.

He was elected Associate of the Royal Academy in 1864, and from this period he began to settle on a theme which would tax him to the full and provide a rich living. This was an individualistic interpretation of classical mythology, where there would be ample scope to show how well he could paint the nude figure. In 1867 appeared his *Venus Disrobing for the Bath* which was, in the jargon of the times, stunning.

His friends could never be sure where he was—Italy, Germany, Egypt, Syria, or Greece. Wherever he went he was treated more as a distinguished ambassador than as an artist, and when he travelled down the Nile it was in the private steam yacht of the country's ruler.

Leighton's fondness for depicting the female form was a source of anxiety to his friends, one of whom was Henry Greville (1801–72), a diplomat and one-time attaché to the embassy in Paris. With reference to Pan and Venus, Greville declared:

If such personages were to be painted, it was not possible to clothe them in crinoline or in green gauze drawers . . . it makes me so sick, all that cant about impropriety, but there is so much of it as to make the sale of 'nude figures' very

A study by Frederic, Lord Leighton, for his painting *Whispers*
in black and white chalk on buff paper. The picture was
exhibited at the Royal Academy in 1881. This study
admirably shows Leighton's method of preparation—the
nude study followed by the clothed version.

improbable, and therefore I hope you will turn your thoughts entirely to well-
covered limbs, and paint no more *Venuses* for some time to come.

It was probable that Greville had seen more than the ice-cool maidens exhibited
at the Royal Academy, but his advice was ignored. When Leighton sent some
paintings to America to be disposed of by Mrs Sartoris's sister, Fanny Kemble, they
were considered so outrageous that they were locked away. In her biography of
Leighton, Mrs Russell Barrington, writing in 1906 when he had been dead less than
a decade and was still a formidable memory in the art world, defended him thus:

In his undraped figures there is the same total absence of the work of the
degenerate as there is in everything he did or was; no remote hint of any *double-
entendre* veiled by aesthetic refinement.

During his lifetime there was gossip about Leighton. He seemed too good to be
true, the handsome bachelor who never formed amatory attachments, who was
always generous to those in need, and who seemed to achieve success so effortlessly.
His house in Melbury Road, Kensington, was one of the marvels of modern

Lord Leighton gave encouragement to many young artists, including Aubrey Beardsley. Although the styles of the two artists are totally different, there is a common element in the unabashed sexuality, urbane and guarded in Leighton, defiant in Beardsley. This is the end piece of Beardsley's illustrations to Oscar Wilde's *Salome*, published in 1894.

London, with its Arabian Court, its indoor fountains, and its rich mosaics, its marble, and its tiles designed by William de Morgan. In the studio was a replica of the frieze of the Parthenon—the battered relic of ancient Greece which had sparked off the enthusiasm for the classical world. Leighton was bringing the background of his paintings indoors and into his own life.

There were accusations that he was homosexual, one of the few charges that could have toppled him from his pedestal, and when one of his favourite boy models, John Hanson Walker, asked Leighton to support his application for a job as a curator there were hints that Walker had some hold over the artist. After the trial of Oscar Wilde in 1895, many men who feared that accusations would shortly be levelled at them left the country hurriedly. It was said that Leighton was one of these, but it is more likely that he was abroad on the grounds of ill-health (and in the event he died shortly afterwards). And there were suggestions that he interfered in some unspecified way with the children he used as models. Mrs Barrington indignantly defended him:

> It is almost unnecessary, as it is distasteful, to mention that this beautiful paternal attitude Leighton displayed towards these orphans [four Miss Pullans] was made the subject of ugly gossip.

Undeterred by rumour and envy, Leighton continued to paint in his own inimitable style. Sometimes there were no nudes, but the pictures which contained naked figures were usually the ones most noted. He also did sculpture. His *Athlete Struggling with a Python* was exhibited at the Royal Academy in 1877, and *Needless Alarms*, a nude girl looking over her shoulder at a frog, dated from 1886, and was presented to Sir John Millais. The sculpture was a spin-off from his painting methods, for he often made models of wax as a prelude to painting a picture.

As prophesied, he became President of the Royal Academy in 1878 and was knighted. Created a baronet in 1886, he was raised to the peerage in 1896 a few days before his death. As President he was truly Olympian, a man come down from Parnassus to tell his humbler colleagues about the meaning of art. To his students he was accessible, and to anxious parents worried about their children enmeshed as pupils in the web of art he wrote consoling and helpful letters. He organized people as he organized his paintings. He professed not to like the business of selling pictures, leaving that to a servant and regarding picture dealers as hardly more than tradesmen, but when the Chantrey Bequest was to be spent he made certain that his own works should be prominent among the pictures purchased.

Sir Francis Chantrey was a grocer's boy who became a rich and flourishing artist, Royal Academician in 1818, and was knighted in 1835. He left £150,000 in Consuls at his death. Except for a life-interest for his wife, the rest of the interest was to be devoted to the purchase of modern British paintings, or sculpture, and it was Leighton's *Athlete Struggling with a Python* which was bought through the Chantrey Bequest in 1879 for £2,000. These acquisitions were destined for a national gallery of British art which did not then exist. (Eventually it came, the Tate Gallery, funded by money from sugar.)

When he died in 1896, Lord Leighton of Stretton, as he briefly was, had a hero's funeral and was buried in St Paul's, with an anthem specially composed by the Director of the Royal College of Music. Swinburne wrote a farewell poem which began:

A light has passed that never shall pass away,
A sun has set whose rays are unequalled of might.

Yet even then there had to be a defence of Leighton's treatment of the figure, and the task was given to the clergy in the person of the Archdeacon of London who in a sermon in Canterbury Cathedral commented that it had been sometimes held that 'devotion to the sense of beauty must necessarily be sensual and lax in moral fibre'. Not so, he went on, for here was this marvellous man whose enthusiasm for 'graceful beauty' was compatible with 'the purest idealism and absence of all that is base or ill-regulated in association'. This unmeaning jumble of words was the closest the clergy could get to voicing their suspicions. Queen Victoria was more honest; although she and Prince Albert had bought Leighton's early *Cimabue* picture, she did not approve of Leighton's style of painting—though the Prince of Wales, later Edward VII, certainly did. He had been a friend of long standing of Leighton.

A retrospective exhibition of Leighton's work shortly after the funeral showed how well a gentleman-artist could acquit himself, and tens of thousands of ordinary people went to the Royal Academy to goggle. Leighton had lived to see his *The Daphnephoris* make £3,937 10s in 1893. (It had been bought by Lord Revelstoke in 1876.) In 1913 the Lever Art Gallery acquired it for £2,625.

After the death of a dominant figure in art there is often a reaction. At the executor's sale in 1896 Leighton's *Perseus and Andromeda*, a popular subject for those who delighted in erotic subjection and suppressed sadism, sold for a mere £651— hardly more than the £630 Queen Victoria paid for *Cimabue*. In 1907 *Golden Hours*, sold for £1,155 in 1888, made only £262 10s. Times had indeed changed, and the fantasies of Frederic Leighton had no place in the motor-car culture of the

Edwardians. To artists who were throwing off the restrictions of Victorianism he was stilted and precious.

Leighton went into a long decline, from which he has only recently emerged. In 1960 the auctioneers Knight, Frank and Rutley sold *The Sargonsian Bride* for £200, a picture for which the dealer Agnew had paid £1,200 in 1866, and which was sold in 1874 for £2,677 10s. The Leightonian excursions into the past had even less relevance to the England of rock'n roll.

Left Leighton had a great influence on other artists and this fine painting by Thomas Armstrong (1835–1911) surely owes much to his work and example. *A Girl Watching a Tortoise* uses classical detail and was exhibited at the Royal Academy in 1874.

Opposite above
The Frigidarium by Laurence Alma-Tadema, painted in 1890. The composition of this picture was regarded by the art critic of *The Athenaeum* as 'exceptionally complex, difficult, and successful'. The nude figures are placed in the background, and caused little concern. In his designs Alma-Tadema shows the influence of Japanese art with its indifference to symmetry.

Opposite below
Although the English nineteenth-century artists were leaders in the evocation of classical times as excuses to portray female nudes, it is clear that they had no monopoly in the re-creation of ancient Rome, Greece, or, when the opportunity arose, Egypt. *The Virgin of the Nile* by Federico Faruffini is an Italian interpretation, and the architecture is reminiscent of that in Alma-Tadema.

Many of the fashionable statues of the 1860s and 1870s have
been relegated to the basements of museums, or broken up,
but this charming statue by G. Lombardi, dated 1867, can be
seen in the courtyard of the White Hart Hotel, Exeter.

7
ALMA-TADEMA,
THE DUTCHMAN

Frederic Leighton's style was nourished on the tight sparsely coloured paintings of the Nazarene school in Germany, in which sheer delight in the manipulation of paint was reduced to a minimum. (One of the leaders claimed that the enemy of their kind of painting was the brush.) He also came under the influence of his Italian masters, and saw the most influential painters of Belgium and Paris at work. He was never subjected to the niggledy disciplines of English art schools, and was free to pick and choose the elements he wanted to weld together and make his own individual style.

Laurens Alma-Tadema also avoided the English system of art teaching by being born in Holland in 1836, and was thus Leighton's junior by a few years. The death of his father at an early age, and the relative poverty of his mother made the chance of a career in art remote, and he went reluctantly into his father's profession, the law, drawing and painting in his spare time. Poor health and the probability that he would not live long led to Alma-Tadema being allowed to study art. The Dutch art schools refused to accept him, so he went over the border into Belgium, and enrolled at the Antwerp Academy.

Since 1830 Belgium had been independent, and was proud of its history, so it was appropriate for art students to attempt historical subjects for the glory of the state. The conditions were very much like those prevalent in Soviet Russia, with the subject supreme. Alma-Tadema became assistant to Hendryk Leys, whose reputation extended outside Belgium. Leys was devoted to the meticulous work of the Dutch and German painters of the past and had an obsession with detail. If there was some doubt about how a piece of furniture looked or how characters in some long-forgotten drama had dressed, Leys or an assistant went to great pains to find out, venturing into archaeology. Leys was a stern teacher, expecting perfection.

Alma-Tadema did not wish to tramp over the same ground as his fellow painters, and went further back in time away from frolicsome costumery into dark unknown ages, where archaeology became speculation and there could be no post-mortem on chairs out of period or a hair style that was anachronistic. His first major success was a picture entitled *The School for Vengeance: The Education of the Children of Clovis* (1861), in which three young children practise the art of hurling the axe in the presence of their widowed mother, who is training them to avenge the murder of their father. It is almost as tedious a subject as Leighton's first big work, but with rather more action.

Nevertheless it had enough patriotic appeal to be bought by the King of the Belgians, but patriotism was not enough and it passed into the hands of Sir John Pender, a pioneer of submarine telegraphy. Alma-Tadema followed this with other works in the same vein, where mayhem and murder were close bed-fellows, but his course was diverted when, in 1863, a promising artist with a good future, he married and went to Italy for his honeymoon. While there he was present during the systematic excavation of Pompeii, submerged intact by volcanic lava in AD 79, and what he saw there was to inspire his future work. The disaster at Pompeii had fired the imagination of the novelist Bulwer-Lytton and in 1834 his novel, *The Last Days of Pompeii*, was a best-seller. There was in consequence an unprecedented interest among the general public in anything to do with ancient Rome.

About this time Alma-Tadema met the French art dealer Ernest Gambart, who was not interested in art for its own sake and markedly indifferent to suffering

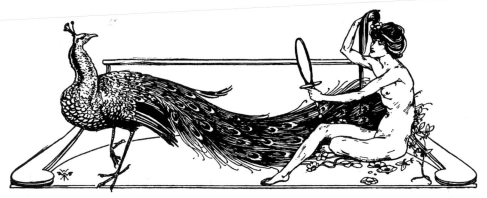

Lawrence Alma-Tadema introduced a slimmer woman into Royal Academy neo-classical painting and this had a significant influence on other artists and on book illustration.

painters. Gambart, with strong connections in England and Europe, was only concerned with the best-selling product—a nineteenth-century media man. He saw in Alma-Tadema someone worth signing up, a master of technique who could turn turgid subjects of the Middle Ages into interesting pictures which would reproduce well in the form of prints. It was soon evident that Alma-Tadema had no aversion to the making of money, whether it was from remote Belgium, Rome in antique times, or ancient Egypt.

It was Egypt—which Alma-Tadema did not visit until late in life—that gave him his first success in the new style, *Egyptians Three Thousand Years Ago*. It was a cunning choice, for the mystery of the Orient was beginning to weave its spell on Europe and, to facilitate tourism, work on the Suez Canal had begun five years earlier, in 1858. A commercial treaty had been signed between Egypt and Britain in 1861, bringing British influence and a certain amount of civilization to the country and the Egyptian cotton trade had begun to blossom.

Alma-Tadema continued to paint Egyptian pictures for more than ten years, but he was more interested in recreating the world of ancient Greece and Rome. The first of his classical period paintings was *Catullus at Lesbia's*, a blameless picture of which a contemporary critic wrote: 'No one had attempted up till then to bring this intimate and personal sentiment into our dreams of the past.' Gradually Alma-Tadema began to incorporate more and more nude women into his pictures, often using the Roman bath as a setting. When the subject did not seem to encourage the inclusion of naked Roman women, Alma-Tadema incorporated naked slave-girls. Slave-girls had a peculiar appeal to the nineteenth century, as they could be depicted bound and handcuffed.

In 1869 Alma-Tadema's first wife died, and he moved from Brussels. He married the daughter of an English doctor and set up house near the Regent's Canal, designing the interior in the Graeco-Roman style. A few years later they moved to St John's Wood, turning an ordinary red-brick house into a palace with verandahs, galleries, porches, and an indoor swimming-pool. The entrance was an exact copy of the doorway of a section of the Forum in Pompeii. Alma-Tadema could refresh his memory by looking through the many thousands of photographs he took on site (photographs that included many naked Italian boys).

With the backing of Gambart, Alma-Tadema had avoided commitment to the tradition represented by the Royal Academy, but in 1876 he was elected an Associate, becoming a full Member three years later. Exposure on the walls of the Royal Academy was not the same as private trading, and although both Alma-Tadema and Leighton belong to the same basic school, their approaches were subtly different. Leighton's nudes were grand, beautifully formed, untouchable and statuesque; Alma-Tadema's were ordinary women, disporting themselves in an everyday way. Not for nothing was Alma-Tadema a Dutchman with a delight in the little intimate details of life. And like Vermeer he could outpaint most.

The Victorian critic Cosmo Monkhouse referred acutely to the Dutch influence in Alma-Tadema's work in his

> . . . preference for interiors and courtyards, with their subtle and complicated effects of reflected light; that wonderful skill in the representation of all kinds of substance and texture, that delight in beautiful colour modified and graduated infinitely by different intensities of illumination, that love of finish and detail . . .

Even Ruskin, for whom a naked woman on canvas seemed a personal challenge, admired Alma-Tadema's skill:

> M. Alma-Tadema differs from all the artists I have ever known, except John Lewis [a painter of Oriental scenes in the most minute detail], in the gradual increase of technical accuracy, which attends and enhances together the expanding range of his dramatic invention; while every year he displays more varied and complex powers of minute draughtsmanship, more especially in architectural detail, wherein, somewhat priding myself as a speciality, I nevertheless receive continual lessons from him.

Nevertheless, when Alma-Tadema affronted him Ruskin could be very fierce indeed, and he called *Pyrrhic Dance* 'gloomy', 'crouching', 'dastardly' (which tells us more about Ruskin's state of mind than the picture itself).

Despite Alma-Tadema's great popularity there were those who considered a naked woman was a naked woman even if she was called Phryne or Andromeda, and in 1879 the Bishop of Carlisle wrote to the painter George Richmond:

> My mind has been considerably exercised this season by the exhibition of Alma-Tadema's nude Venus. [There might] be artistic reasons which justify such public exposure of the female form . . . In the case of the nude of an Old Master such allowance can be made, but for a living artist to exhibit a life-size, life-like, almost photographic representation of a beautiful naked woman strikes my inartistic mind as somewhat if not very mischievous.

Naturally the Bishop of Carlisle did not flourish a cheque book and his comments, if expressed publicly, could increase interest in a picture. Certainly Alma-Tadema did not heed the bishop's warning, even had he heard of it, and in 1881 one of his most luscious nudes, *In the Tepidarium*, made its appearance at the Royal Academy, frankly sexual with something of the uncompromising take-it-or-leave-it air of an eighteenth-century Boucher. As with all Alma-Tadema's work, it

Even more than Lord Leighton, Alma-Tadema made neo-classical settings acceptable to ordinary people through the many prints which were made from his paintings. When advertising Vogeler's Curative Compound ('Prepared in England by English People') it seemed to the designer an appropriate style.

Alma-Tadema and his fellow neo-classical Academicians
had a significant effect on women's dress, bringing about the
revival of loose-fitting robes which could be draped
revealingly. This influence was helped by the enthusiasm for
what was known as 'Rational Dress'.

is signed with an opus number; as this was opus 229, it gives some idea of the
fertility of the artist, and there was much more to come, for Alma-Tadema
continued to paint until his death in 1912.

The presence or absence of nudes does not seem to have greatly affected Alma-
Tadema's popularity, and his chaste and serene *An Apodyterium* was voted the best
picture of 1886. As he got older Alma-Tadema became less keen on historical
accuracy, and if he wanted to paint hollyhocks, as he did in his fine 1886 picture, he
did not bother to check whether they were extant in classical Rome nor, in *Anthony
and Cleopatra* of 1883, did he concern himself about the old English roses which
stretch across the canopy over Cleopatra.

There were no complications about Lawrence (he anglicized his name in 1873
when he became a naturalized Englishman) Alma-Tadema. His married life was
happy, he was not obsessed with his art as Etty was, and his philosophy was simple:

Art is imagination, and those who love Art love it because in looking at a picture
it awakens their imagination and sets them thinking; and that is also why Art
heightens the mind.

Unlike Leighton, Alma-Tadema did not induce feelings of awe, and his
hospitality was famous. A plump little man with a beard and pince-nez, he was
extrovert and companionable. In 1899 he was knighted, and was much liked by
King Edward VII, who awarded him the Order of Merit, the monarch's
prerogative. It is said that this was a reward for painting a series of pornographic
murals at Windsor Castle.

He had a book of poetry published, was a clever photographer, an accomplished musician who won the friendship of Paderewski and was involved in theatre production. Association with Henry Irving resulted in Alma-Tadema providing moonlight effects for *Coriolanus* in 1880 using electric light. As a business man he was astute, though he complained that he never earned more than £10,000 a year (£200,000, almost tax-free, in modern money). It is said that Gambart paid £10,000 for *The Roman Picture Gallery* in 1874, which included the copyright on the picture. This was important, for it meant that Gambart could make a good deal of money by marketing prints from the picture. Alma-Tadema was not averse to this procedure, unlike Leighton who thought that a print from a picture was an indifferent thing and reflected badly not only on the picture itself but on the crass materialism of the artist. Unquestionably, only the vaguest idea can be obtained of Alma-Tadema's paintings from prints, for much of his effect lay in his lighting and his exemplary colour sense.

As with Leighton, Alma-Tadema's prices plunged in the years following his death, a low point being reached in 1960—when the art world was spending tens of thousands of pounds on an American abstract-expressionist picture which probably took less than half an hour to paint. *Roses of Elagabalus* by Alma-Tadema, commissioned for £4,000 in 1888, sold at Christie's for £105.

Above all, Leighton, Alma-Tadema and Poynter were professionals, but the Pre-Raphaelites, especially Rossetti, made Bohemianism fashionable, and in the 1880s the free-living free-loving artist who painted scantily dressed girls for the sheer pleasure of it became a contemporary hero.

8

POYNTER,
THE PROFESSIONAL

The third of the painters who reconstructed ancient life to appeal to Victorian audiences, Edward John Poynter, was a rather more mysterious figure. There are few problems about either Leighton or Alma-Tadema. They are all of a piece, consistent in their zeal, Leighton so intent on upholding the prestige and dignity of the Royal Academy, Alma-Tadema the apostle of commonsense, not caring whether he did deals with Gambart or other picture dealers, exhibited at the Royal Academy, or showed his pictures off at the new Grosvenor Gallery. Poynter on the other hand is more difficult to pin down, a fugitive figure.

The one thing Leighton, Alma-Tadema and Edward John Poynter have in common is that they were, by any standards—even Victorian standards which expected a man to be a jack of all trades and master of them all—extraordinarily accomplished in a variety of pursuits. They were not only a cut above the ordinary artists, but above most men. Poynter was, if anything, more versatile than his contemporaries, for he carried on a selection of careers at the same time, and they were demanding occupations which would have been full-time jobs for most people.

Poynter was born in 1836, the son of a very successful architect whose public buildings are still with us, for better rather than for worse. Westminster School, noted for its coarse bullying, was no place for the delicate quiet lad, and he was sent to Brighton College for a year, before moving on to Ipswich Grammar School. His health was still poor, so he went with a tutor to Madeira, then on to Rome in 1853, where he became friendly with Leighton, who was the toast of society in Rome, and although only twenty-three his poise and general air of culture awed Poynter.

Although having had lessons in water-colour painting from the topographical artist Thomas Shotter Boys, Poynter had no driving ambition to become a professional painter, but with Leighton's encouragement he was fired to enthusiasm, allowed to use his senior's studio and equipment, and although he did not stay in Rome for long he returned to England firmly convinced that painting was his forte—the kind of grand painting practised by Leighton.

There was no objection by his parents to Poynter's enrolling in Leigh's Academy in Newman Street, one of the many schools run by not very talented artists who had failed to make a living by the practice of their craft. Its limitations were evident to the innocent Poynter, and he became a pupil in the studio of William Dobson (1817–98), the Hamburg-born son of an English merchant who had once taught at the Birmingham School of Design, and who was in 1855 to have a picture of his admired by Queen Victoria. He is something of a curiosity in that he was not elected to the Royal Academy until he was fifty-five, and in that he outlived Leighton.

Dobson, too, failed to fit the bill, and Poynter enrolled at the Royal Academy Schools, where the teaching was hide-bound and boring and the teachers were without enthusiasm. Visiting Paris for the Universal Exposition of 1855, Poynter decided that if he wanted to learn art this was the place, and an uncle advised him to see Charles Gleyre, a very able artist who was carrying on the classical revival in France.

Art historians have persisted in finding Gleyre a comic figure, or if not comic, picturesque. He was the ultimate of perfectionists, and before putting pencil to paper or brush to canvas he meditated, often for years. A canvas could wait for months on an easel while Gleyre worked out the next stroke. As a young man he

A study for a nymph by Edward Poynter, showing his
mastery of the female nude. The note of suppressed
eroticism often found in Poynter's work is absent in his
innumerable studies.

had spent four years in frenzied study, followed by four years' inertia in Italy,
succeeded by six adventurous wandering years in Greece, Egypt, the Sudan and
Syria, and was then struck down by fever, which was compounded by eye trouble.
He returned to Paris, prematurely aged, took a studio, and began to paint two
decorative panels, *Diana Leaving the Bath* and a *Young Nubian*, the titles of which
announce Gleyre's forte—the painting of nudes.

They were ignored, and he opened his account with the public in the Salon—the
French equivalent of the Royal Academy—in 1840 with his *Apocalyptic Vision of St
John*. He rarely exhibited his work and after 1849, never. He was devoted to his art,
scorning the applause of the mass public and not wanting wealth. He adored
painting women, but individually detested them. He took pupils, but refused to
take any fee from them.

Many of the great Impressionist artists of the nineteenth century passed
through Gleyre's large grimy studio, reacting against his meticulous detail and his
revulsion against anything that was impulsive. The imaginative could also see
something sinister in the women he painted and the situations in which they were
set, as though the hatred of women was coming through, suppressed under the
immaculate painterly surface. But not so Poynter; he absorbed the Gleyre ethic
from 1856 to 1859 and, being far more impressionable than Leighton, he was not
able to select the elements which most agreed with him.

While in Paris he was an amiable member of what was described as the 'Paris
Gang'—English and American students (including the American, Whistler, who

shared an apartment with Poynter) who had decided that Paris was the place to be for it was cheap, exciting, and far away from parental influence. There were Paris gangs until the start of World War II, for accommodation remained cheaper than in England, with vast studios waiting to be let at less than two pounds a week. In Paris Leighton renewed his friendship with Poynter, and Poynter was also friendly with George du Maurier, the cartoonist of *Punch* and soon to be famous on account of his novel *Trilby* with its sinister mesmerist Svengali. Poynter appears in *Trilby* along with his assorted colleagues, as does the studio of Gleyre. Poynter visited Antwerp with du Maurier, and returned to Britain, sending a painting to the Royal Academy. This was rejected in 1860, but accepted in 1862 (though 'skied'—put up high on the walls; the favoured place was 'the line', an imaginary line extending round the gallery seven foot up).

There was thus no fanfare for Poynter, no talk of him as the coming man, no approaches from the dealer Gambart, and somewhat depressed he looked elsewhere for employment. He found it with William Burges, an architect fiercely involved in what was known as the War of the Styles, between Classical building and Gothic building. The Gothic style, with its own prophet, John Ruskin, was more exciting, and was to reach its zenith with St Pancras Station and Hotel, still with us to startle the eye. Burges (1827–81) was more Gothic than most, with a refreshing enthusiasm for sharply contrasting textures and colours. Responsible for Cork Cathedral, his masterpiece was his exotic recreation of Cardiff Castle. Poynter worked with him in restoration work on Waltham Abbey and in doing some murals, and he was also involved in designing panels for Burges's Gothic cabinets. Poynter did some stained glass too, an art form that had received powerful momentum from the demand for new churches, to cater for the growing populations of the industrial cities.

For a man who could turn his hand to such varied kinds of applied art there was plenty of work available. He was commissioned by the brothers Dalziel, a famous family of engravers, to supply illustrations for a picture Bible, concentrating on the life of Joseph. He continued to paint pictures for the Royal Academy, mainly on Egyptian themes, as Alma-Tadema was doing, and in his 1866 contribution, *Israel in Egypt*, he scored a huge success. As with Leighton's first Royal Academy offering, the *Procession*, Poynter used a frieze-like approach, but his picture has an air of life and animation, and is full of realistic touches. His painting of architecture was never to be as breath-taking as that of Alma-Tadema, but it stood up well to scrutiny, and his pictures had the advantage of being understood at a glance.

With Leighton's picture few observers would have realized that Cimabue was a renowned early Italian painter, but no one could have missed the point of *Israel in Egypt*, with captive Israelites hauling a huge sculpture. In case there was a chance of its Biblical inspiration being missed, Poynter had appended a quotation from Exodus. The picture was bought by Sir John Hawkshaw, an engineer, who had built bridges and railways at Cannon Street and Charing Cross, and had a personal interest in pulling large objects about. He maintained that there were not enough Israelites to move the sculpture, and to accommodate him Poynter repainted part of the picture to extend the line of slaves out of the edge of the painting, so that those who were worried about the logistics could add extra men at will.

During this period he became acquainted with Edward and Georgiana Burne-

Jones. Burne-Jones (1833–98) was a second-phase Pre-Raphaelite painter, seeking a dream world far from the hurly-burly of Victorian England, and he and his wife lived in Great Russell Street opposite the British Museum. Poynter took over their quarters, and married Mrs Burne-Jones's sister Agnes in 1866.

Primitive engineering also featured in Poynter's next major picture, *The Catapult*, an imaginative reconstruction of the rock-throwing Roman machine used at the siege of Carthage, and this guaranteed his election as an Associate of the Royal Academy. The subject was above reproach, and it was painted with great skill. There was less certainty among the critics about the next pictures Poynter was to paint, for he became fascinated by the mythology of Andromeda. This involved a nude woman tied up and in distress, and was the subject guaranteed to make clergymen hot under their dog-collars.

A figure of *Andromeda* alone was exhibited at the Royal Academy in 1870, but the subsequent trio of Andromeda, the rescuer Perseus, and the monster, appeared in 1872. There were ready buyers for all paintings on the Andromeda theme, and these included the Earl of Wharncliffe, who commissioned an Andromeda along with three other paintings from Poynter, *The Fight between More and More Hall and the Dragon of Wantley, Atlanta's Race,* and *Nausicaa and her Maidens Playing at the Ball.* These were to decorate the walls of the Earl's billiard room.

Perseus and Andromeda put the critics in a dilemma to which, since Leighton's nudes, they had been accustomed—how to demonstrate their unease and yet retain their composure. Resemblances were seen to the work of Burne-Jones, but the Poynter work had an intensity and a mastery of light and shade that owed more to the work of his master Gleyre, and an overall design that echoed, at a distance, Michelangelo. The critics tamely complained that the hero, though elegant, lacked heroic proportions and, said the *Art Journal*, was 'utterly incapable of coping with the beast'. It is possible that their attention was so diverted by the splendid nude occupying the left-hand side of the picture that they failed to see that Perseus was well capable of delivering summary justice on the monster and had, indeed, a sword down the creature's gaping throat.

Perhaps because he felt that the life of a professional painter was too uncertain, Poynter became in 1871 the first Slade Professor at University College, London, proving that his cardinal qualities had been noted. His inaugural address was no mere catalogue of platitudes. He praised the French method of art teaching and advised students to study the Old Masters, especially the Italians, as a study of English paintings would be worthless. He was not impressed by the Royal Academy Schools and later, in 1886, he wrote to *The Times* mentioning that he had 'never met an Academy student who does not say that he stops at the Academy Schools because he cannot leave for Paris'.

Proof of the half-hearted way in which the Academy approached teaching is that between 1852 and 1867 the post of Professor of Painting lay vacant, with no enthusiasm on the part of the Academy to see it filled. The President of the Royal Academy during most of this period was Sir Charles Eastlake who was never too busy to write a book on art history or painting in oils. No one however could have accused Poynter of being lax. In 1874 he became Director of the South Kensington Schools (now the Royal College of Art), and by virtue of this office also supervisor of the principal art schools outside London. He ordered a review of their teaching

Edward Poynter's *Perseus and Andromeda*, illustrative of the
Victorian fondness for seeing women bound and helpless.
The critic of the *Art Journal* complained that Perseus was
'utterly incapable of coping with the beast' and averted his
eyes from Andromeda. It is interesting to compare
Poynter's rendering with Bell's sculpture of Andromeda.

methods, the main tenet of which was the institution of the life class and drawing
from the nude. Many artists who were taught at provincial art colleges have much
to thank Poynter for, for without a lead from above puritanical and prudish local
councils would have been reluctant to introduce such methods.

Although Poynter was now a person of some prominence, with more power in
the art world at grass-roots level, though indirectly, than a President of the Royal
Academy had or was ever likely to have, this did not stop him being rapped over the
knuckles by Ruskin when *The Golden Age* was exhibited in 1875. At this time Ruskin
was Slade Professor of Fine Art at Oxford, clearly half-mad, and talking thorough
nonsense to his bemused students. Of *The Golden Age*, Ruskin wrote:

> *The Golden Age* in this pinchbeck one interests nobody. Not even the painter—
> for had he looked at the best authorities for an account of it, he would have found
> that its people lived chiefly on corn and strawberries both growing wild; and
> doubtless the loaded fruit-branches drooped to their reach.

This sarcastic mumbling would have impressed few and puzzled most, but his
next volley was more acute: the picture appeared to 'savour somewhat of
adventitious gas-lighting', and while the painter aimed 'to show us like
Michelangelo, the adaptability of limbs to awkward positions . . . he can only, by
this anatomical science, interest his surgical spectators'. No doubt Ruskin was distressed by Poynter's use of deep shadow, for paintings which contained darkness
upset him almost as much as storm clouds, seeing which could drive him into mania.

Yet, despite his prejudices, Ruskin was observant. Poynter's figures did throw
themselves about, whether they were clothed or nude, and his women were often
prone and languid in a curious but sensual way, not often seen in Leighton or Alma-
Tadema although it was common in French paintings of the time.

Poynter often developed his nudes at the water's-edge, and the
mermaid was a popular subject for Royal Academicians
during his period as President. "You meet her in Homer
and you meet her in Tennyson", enthused the *Magazine of
Art* in 1883, "on the coasts of legendary Hellas and in the
waters round the Isle of Wight" (surely of interest for
visitors to Cowes). This interpretation is by Otto Sinding.

Poynter's tone of suppressed sexuality is echoed here in Frederick Sandys's *Danaë in the Brazen Chamber*, engraved about 1865, and rejected by the editor of the mazagine *Once a Week* as being too sensual. Danaë had never seen a man, and was haunted by the appearance of Jove, of whom she is weaving the tapestry (seen on the left of the picture). Sandys (1832–1904) refused to amend his engraving when asked by the editor.

Unlike many artists attacked by Ruskin, Poynter had a platform on which to fight back — the lecture rostrum. He went straight for the jugular, Ruskin's aversion to the human figure. The 'glory of nature and God's works' meant to Ruskin 'mossy rocks and birds' nests . . . robin red-breasts, anything you like, in fact, but the figure for its beauty'. Nor did Ruskin's hostility have much effect on the Poynter market; he always sold, even when he did not command the highest sums. His *Diadumene*, a life-size nude which was exhibited at the Royal Academy in 1884, did attract criticism but was sold when Poynter had added some drapery — whereupon it went to the United States.

A smart soldierly figure, shy beneath an air of aloofness, Poynter found no need to change his style or his subject matter. He resigned as Director of the South Kensington Schools in 1881, and it reverted to sloth and inactivity. In 1894 the directorship of the National Gallery became vacant and Poynter was given the job, soon proving that he was more than equal to the challenge, holding the post until 1905. One of his greatest achievements was his editing of the *Illustrated Catalogue of the National Gallery*, in which every picture in the collection is reproduced. He also made some very good buys on behalf of the nation, particularly the *Agony in the Garden* by Mantegna (1431–1506).

In 1896 he was made President of the Royal Academy, and remained so until 1918. This was remarkable but perhaps unfortunate for, although Poynter had extraordinarily catholic taste regarding artists of the past, he was steadfastly against the advanced paintings of the time, and especially Impressionism. He claimed that Impressionist painters neglected the study of form 'in favour of so-called impressions, hastily, and more or less dextrously, thrown on canvas'. The Impressionists shirked the labour and difficulties of the study of the form; they were incompetent in drawing and slovenly in execution.

Of course, none of this was true, but Poynter could not betray the principles of a life time, and many of his contemporaries agreed with him, though a Degas, grouped by the supporters of Impressionism with Manet and Renoir, was sold to the British collector, Louis Huth, as early as 1872. A Paris dealer, Durand-Ruel, had set up a gallery at 168 New Bond Street in 1870 for the exposure of Impressionist and other French artists, but the project was unsuccessful. Later, in 1883, Durand-Ruel set up an exhibition of sixty-five works at Dowdeswell's Galleries, and although the establishment papers (such as *The Times* and *Punch*) thought it hilarious many critics gave close attention to the paintings. With the British love of figure painting and the picture which told a story it is hardly surprising that Manet, Renoir and Degas were the most popular, while Monet puzzled almost all. But those with a long memory and a sense of history recalled the days when the landscapes of Constable and Turner were greeted with contempt.

Poynter, predictably knighted when he became President of the Royal Academy, and made a baronet in 1902, lived through the early days of Cubism and even the beginnings of abstract art, but whether he noticed them is a matter for speculation. Under him, the Edwardian Royal Academy was not a whit different from the Victorian Royal Academy, with the same artists sending in their predictable work, and these included the President himself.

Time had not affected the ambiguous, subtly erotic and mysterious tone of Poynter's paintings. Towards the end of his life, Leighton had tended to paint fewer nudes, but not Poynter. With one or two possible exceptions they were the most suggestive paintings in the annual exhibitions. In the 1902 exhibition he put in *Storm Nymphs*, and in 1904 there was *The Sea Cave*, a decidedly odd painting, and *Astérie*, notable for its transparent draperies. And such works were to continue, all assiduously prepared with careful preliminary sketches.

Over the years the Elgin Marbles had begun to lose their unique stature, and the eagerness with which the classical world was reinterpreted had been lost. A vague mythology had persisted, with standard themes being repeated year in and year out, and on the fringe of this mythology in a sort of Celtic twilight worked Poynter and his followers and imitators.

It is interesting to ponder on the possible effect a man of a different cast might have had on the Royal Academy in the period leading up to World War I. Would the Royal Academy have made some attempt to come to terms with modern times?

9
THE ART MARKET

High Art would not have existed for very long if it had been too lofty for the market. The term was accepted gratefully by the practitioners, for it had the same sort of connotation as, for example, an 'official' programme. Its purpose was to express universal values and unquestioned morals, to show that even among the bad there was an element of goodness. In Poynter's *Israel in Egypt*, for example, an Egyptian is depicted giving water to a captive Israelite. Spectators enjoyed the warm feeling of knowing that despite a gap of two thousand years people were very much the same—or so the painters of High Art led them to believe.

High Art was not only moral art, but also instructional. Who would have thought that the boring characters in almost-forgotten school primers were flesh and blood, and were so full of human interest? High Art was also flattering to rich buyers. Britain was the logical successor to ancient Rome, and parallels could be drawn almost at random with the certainty that somehow they would be pertinent. Rome had the greatest empire, Rome had a taste for high living, Rome had beautiful

Philip Calderon (1833–98) is best known as a historical painter. An Associate of the Royal Academy in 1864, Royal Academician in 1867, he became Keeper of the Royal Academy in 1887. *St Elizabeth of Hungary* is perhaps the most erotic of all Victorian Academy paintings.

women and vigorous men, Rome had magnificent buildings. The *pax Romanica* was hardly different to the age of Victoria, and this illusion could be kept up if one did not glance at the seamier side of life.

The seamier side of life had its painters too, and if low characters could be made picturesque and quaint there was a rich vein of ore for artists to mine; many first-class painters did not need to step outside the boundaries of genre painting and both genre painters and High Art painters made use of the popularity of paintings with stories.

Their competitors were the specialists in landscape, marine artists and, naturally, the portrait artists, though most of the masters of High Art did not consider it beneath their dignity to paint portraits of the rich or the famous, and preferably both. Many of Leighton's earlier works were portraits, mostly of people now forgotten, like the Countess Cowley, the Hon Frederick Wellesley, the Bentinck family, Lady Pollington and Lady Charlotte Greville.

Whatever style an artist practised he could make certain of a worthwhile career if he kept an eye on the potential buyer. The buyers were not all of the same class, and the only common denominator was that they all had surplus wealth. The aristocracy always provided their share of buyers, but they were often less important than the new rich, many of whom had risen from common workmen to tycoons in a few years and whose ignorance of art and culture in general was often total. They knew what they liked, without knowing why, and with equal emphasis they knew what they disliked, and were indifferent to the great painters of the past.

Their preferences could be astonishing and parochial. David Cox (1783–1859) was a capable landscape artist, and because he was a local man the industrialists of Birmingham decided that he ought to be supported. A water-colour which was sold for £6 6s in 1840 was resold in 1870 for £433. Joseph Gillott, on the other hand, the pen-maker from Edgbaston, bought Turners and many of the water-colours in his collection went up by eighty times between the 1830s and the 1890s.

There were many capable artists who copied other men's styles simply because they were in fashion. Sir Augustus Wall Callcott (1777–1844) is best known for his story-book pictures, and *Blind Milton Dictating to his Daughters* (1840) was reproduced by the tens of thousands and can be seen still on the walls of middle-class families. But Callcott made his money from imitation Turners.

Joseph Gillott was typical of the industrial patron. Born in 1799, he was a working cutler in Sheffield before he removed to Birmingham in 1821. He there found employment in the 'steel toy trade', the name given to the manufacture of steel buckles, chains and ornamental steel-work. About 1830 he turned his attention to the production of steel pens by machinery, and built up a thriving business.

Elhanan Bicknell was another industrialist who bought Turner, often paying considerable sums of money for choice works. A schoolmaster's son, Bicknell had realized that there was a rapidly growing market for whale-oil for lamps and had made a fortune from this source. He began collecting in 1838 when he was fifty, and at the time of his death he had a collection at his Newington Butts home of 145 pictures. Never a collector on the scale of Gillott (whose collection of 525 pictures was auctioned at Christie's in 1872), he was nevertheless a valuable patron. He once offered Turner £35,000 for the entire contents of the short-lived Turner Gallery in Queen Anne Street, London, an offer which was refused.

The tastes of E. J. Colman, the mustard king, were more extrovert. In 1881 his executors sold three Landseers at more than £5,000 each, including one which Landseer had dashed off in three hours in Colman's house and sent to the Royal Academy just as it was. One of the other Landseer buyers was Thomas Holloway, famous for his patent medicines, who wanted pictures to adorn one of his philanthropic projects, a women's college at Egham near Virginia Water. Holloway was immensely wealthy (and way ahead of his time in his appreciation of the value of advertising, on which he spent £50,000 a year).

Other collectors included T. E. Plint, a stockbroker from Leeds, the ironmaster Bolckow, and the Manchester calico-printer, Edmund Potter. Joseph Ruston, the manufacturer of agricultural machinery, was not averse to speculation, and bought the works of Rossetti, while George McCulloch spent £200,000 on modern art. McCulloch was one of the most dashing of entrepreneurs, winning the Broken Hill gold-mine in Australia at a game of cards, but he often paid too much and when his acquisitions came up for auction they made less than he paid for them.

The time of the Great Exhibition of 1851 marked a turning point in prices. Up to that point there were only four or five painters who could command £1,000 a picture. Twenty-five years later, and £4,000 a picture was not out of the way. Most buyers were careful—unlike Gillott and Bicknell, who followed their own fancy. Although they took expert advice they were often obliged to pay more than they should have because of the machinations of dealers. The innocent businessmen and industrialists, so shrewd in their own affairs, were 'marks', and they could be 'run up' in the sale room by the vendors, or agents operating for the vendors.

There was strong competition from dealers, such as Gambart, who were not so much interested in the picture itself but in the copyright of it, so that prints could be made. An imitator of the grand style, Edwin Long, could command more than the genuine artist. Long's *The Babylonian Marriage Market* from the Royal Academy Exhibition of 1875 sold privately to Edward Hermon MP for £7,350, and seven years later it was sold for £6,615, a record sale-room price for a living English artist. It was bought by Thomas Holloway for his women's college, no doubt to demonstrate to impressionable young ladies what their fate could be if they said yes too often.

While living Royal Academicians flourished, the Old Masters were doing rather badly, with Titians and van Eycks going for less than the most mediocre pot-boiler, and only Raphael keeping his values. In the 1870s and 1880s John Millais (1829–96) was making between £25,000 and £40,000 a year with his exquisitely painted, brightly coloured pictures. To keep such figures in perspective, it is worth while remembering that a skilled craftsman such as a carpenter or a stone-mason earned between £75 and £100 a year (official 1880 figures), and that a rich man paid less than 5 per cent of his income in taxes.

Millais is the prime example of an artist who gauged the taste of the buying public to a tee. This was recognized by those anxious to cash in on the boom in contemporary painting. *Cherry Ripe* of 1879, a portrait of a little girl, was presented in a colour reproduction in the *Graphic* in 1880, and 600,000 were sold. A picture of a small boy blowing bubbles from a clay pipe was bought by Sir William Ingram for the *Illustrated London News* to be reproduced in chromolithography, since the 1840s the most successful method of printing in full colour. The reproduction was seen by

A Roman Bath by Edwin Douglas, dated 1899, is a frankly
erotic painting, and it is interesting that as late as this many
painters found it necessary to place their nudes in a
historical setting to deflect criticism.

This Berlin plaque of the late nineteenth century
demonstrates that the nude figure could be illustrated in a
wide variety of mediums and that interpretations varied
little from country to country, though the pair of wings may
be a peculiarly Prussian touch.

the manager of Pears Soap, who bought the copyright. For many years Pears Soap was associated with *Bubbles*, and *Bubbles* with Pears Soap. Art was being brought to the masses in a big way.

The painters of the neo-classical school shared in the wealth being distributed, and it was McCulloch, the magnate of the Broken Hill gold-mine, who bought one of Leighton's most luscious nudes. There was momentary alarm when a severe trade recession occurred between 1884 and 1887, but this did not seem to affect the buying of modern British paintings for, although private buyers were more subdued, the dealers continued to spend heavily and the market for reproductions was as strong as ever.

Most hurt by the 1884–7 slump was agriculture. Wheat prices, the key to agricultural prosperity, had dropped alarmingly, from 56s 9d in 1877 to 31s 6d in 1886. This was a direct result of the import of cheap American grain following the opening up of the West and the prairies. Train and steamship brought the grain to Britain, and by 1880 65 per cent of all the grain used in Britain came from the United States. British farmers suffered, of course, but farmers had been inured to good and bad years and accepted the disasters philosophically or left for the towns.

The great landowners were shattered. Farmers could not afford to pay them their rents, and holdings became derelict. Many of the landowners were desperate and could not see a way to survive, except by selling off family treasures. Many noble collections were sent to London for auction. The slump coincided with the emergence of a new buying class—the American millionaires, unaffected by the recession, and having incomparable wealth to spread around, if the mood took them. As with the British industrialists, they knew what they liked, and what they liked particularly were French paintings, whether they were the soft landscapes of Corot (1796–1875) or the saucy pictures of Bouguereau (1825–1905). Competition between American millionaires and French buyers sent the values of French contemporary painting (except for the Impressionists and anything that savoured of adventure) through the roof. The Americans were even keen on the French school known as 'the Dismals'—gloom among the peasantry, dauntingly realistic and painted in muddy colours. (The best known of the Dismals was Millet, whose picture *The Angélus* became probably the most famous painting in the world. It found its way to the Louvre at 800,000 francs or £32,000.)

The British art world gaped and wondered. The home market was stable enough, but the men who were buying British were turning their attentions to French rivals, especially Meissonier (1815–91), whose main preoccupation was seeing how much minute detail he could pack into a painting. Shrewd picture-buyers had a good reason for going into French pictures for, despite a buoyant Royal Academy, many businessmen had backed the wrong horses, and found that when they wanted to resell they were forced to do so at a loss. The vast money being spent on Meissonier and his ilk also persuaded the rich British buyer that they must be good.

When the Americans turned their attention to British art treasures they did not, as many supposed, go for the High Art pictures, neo-classical nudes, or for pictures which told a story. They concentrated on portraits, and the portraits of the past. Almost single-handed, Rothschild had restored Gainsborough to the best-seller list, and the fashion for buying portraits of ancestors of total strangers led to fierce competition, not between the dealers, the British private buyers, and the Europeans, but between four American millionaires, Pierpont Morgan, P.A.B. Widener, Benjamin Altman, and Henry Clay Frick. In 1906 Van Dyck became the highest-priced painter in the world, when a portrait by him sold for £103,300. The portrait mania lasted until the 1920s, and there is still a vogue for old portraits, of any standard, that can masquerade as an ancestor.

During the time of the slump, the dramatic entry of the Americans into the art scene, and the astonishing popularity of modern French art, Leighton was President of the Royal Academy, hardly seeming to be aware of the events happening outside, and more intent on preserving the image of the Royal Academy and in fighting off snipers. In the first year of his Presidency, about four hundred thousand people visited the summer exhibition, with gate money of over £20,000. Criticism of the Royal Academy was loudly voiced on account of its power. It was a private institution exercising great influence on the picture-buying public. Academicians had the right to exhibit eight paintings, outsiders no rights at all; outsiders were at the mercy of the Hanging Committee, who picked what they themselves liked.

The Academy was attacked in Parliament, and Leighton and Gladstone were obliged to cobble up some kind of answer to these onslaughts. Walter Crane published a letter in the *Pall Mall Gazette* calling attention to the 'irresponsible power' and 'corrupting influence' of the Royal Academy. Harry Quilter, art critic of *The Times*, spoke of its 'feebleness, frivolity, and melodrama'. Leighton himself kept outside the conflict, but it did not help the cause of the Academy that many of the most talented artists refused to exhibit there, including the Pre-Raphaelites Holman Hunt and Rossetti, Whistler and Burne-Jones, though peace was made with Burne-Jones and he did exhibit one picture at the Royal Academy.

Although other galleries opened in London throughout the nineteenth century—and Leighton was always encouraging them, spending a good deal of time on the South London Art Gallery, and making periodic contributions of the odd hundred pounds from his own pocket—the Royal Academy was the premier showplace. A picture on its walls misleadingly gave confidence to a prospective buyer, and there was great snob value in obtaining a picture from a summer exhibition. (The winter exhibitions were minor affairs with poor gate money.)

Of course, there was no reason why a Royal Academy picture should be any more worthy than one in, say, the Grosvenor Gallery. It was more likely that one would see worse pictures, simply because an Academician could put in a flop to make his number up. No one knows what sort of pictures were turned away disdainfully by the Hanging Committee.

Pictures could, and can, be seen in a variety of lights. They can be status symbols; a portrait can be assigned to an ancestor by someone who wished to pretend that he was, if not of noble birth, at least a descendant of someone of consequence. The nude and suggestive paintings could be smokers' den and billiard-room pictures or even bedroom pictures. They could be investments, or they could simply be liked, perhaps because they reminded the owner of pleasant scenes and memories, or because they told a charming and well-known story.

The artist was helped by a fashion among the well-off middle classes for cramming pictures into every available wall space, from skirting board to picture

A modest middle-of-the-road semi-nude by J. W. Schofield,
interesting because it is clearly a contemporary girl in a
contemporary setting, with no pretence of its all taking
place in ancient Rome.

The copyrights of suitable pictures were often bought by
firms to advertise their products (the most obvious example
being the purchase of the copyright of *Bubbles* by Pears).
Sometimes the firms used their own designs, as
in this bath scene.

rail until the wallpaper or panelling could hardly be seen. In the massive houses of
the nineteenth century there was plenty of wall space. The servants' quarters in the
basements or attics did not warrant paintings, but these were the ideal places to
deposit acquisitions which were temporarily out of favour or to hang prints.

On the other hand, the artist was handicapped by the increase in the mobility of
paintings and therefore in competition. In the old picture-collecting families it was
usual to hand the pictures down from generation to generation and they rarely came
under the hammer. The agricultural recession had pushed many of these pictures
into the auction house. The industrialists and businessmen who had been busy
buying paintings throughout the century did not, as it is clear from the number of
executors' sales of their collections, hand their treasures down to sons and
daughters. Perhaps pictures by living artists had been out of circulation for a few
years; they were now on the open market again, and although it was gratifying for
an artist if his prices had gone up in the interim there was no money to be made out
of this for him. If, as often happened, the prices were lower it could not only depress
a painter mentally but depress him financially when it came for him to sell his latest
work.

Some painters held to the maxim 'art for art's sake'. This was, in some cases,
self-defence against the laws of supply and demand which could make or destroy.
Often those with the biggest purses had more money than sense but, fortunately for
some of the most talented painters, it was not always true.

10
BURNE-JONES,
THE ARTIST
IN DREAMLAND

The art world of London was a closely knit circle, and even when there were differences of opinion there was a general concern to present a united front to the public at large. (In Britain today so many artists and groups of artists work in hermetically sealed units, contemptuous of outside rivals following totally distinct paths, their work often difficult to class under the heading of art.)

In the nineteenth century, most art was capable of being understood by the man in the street. There was a subject of some kind, and the artist interpreted it. Sometimes the way it was interpreted was not liked, sometimes actively disliked. When Whistler (1834–1903) etched and painted his impressions of London, taking more interest in the atmosphere and feeling than in representation, it was clear to see what his intention was, and although critics pretended that he was wilfully obscure, the characteristic they particularly disliked was what they considered his lack of finish. They were also resentful because he gave his works airy titles, often taken from music, such as *Nocturne*, and charged what were considered extravagant prices.

The acrimony between Whistler and the chief art critic of the time, John Ruskin, resulted in a court case which helped no one, as it opened up to the public cracks in artists' unity which had until then been carefully papered over. Technically, Whistler won the lawsuit, being awarded a farthing's damages, but he was financially crippled by the costs of the case. Artists were recruited for witnesses, often to their distress by being aligned against friends in the opposite camp, and the only people who were at all happy about the general unpleasantness were the critics who had a wonderful opportunity to air their prejudices in public.

For artists themselves, the biggest talking point was whether to be in the Royal Academy or remain outside it. Most of the artists who did not exhibit at the Royal Academy—and we are not speaking of the incompetents who have disappeared for ever into the past—could have exhibited there had they wished, but for one reason or another they preferred to remain outside, either because they found the atmosphere of the Royal Academy cloying and incestuous, or because they resented the privilege enjoyed by the Academy and the Academicians.

Two very important painters who for most of their lives remained outside the Royal Academy were Edward Burne-Jones and George Frederick Watts. Their attitude towards the nude figure was totally different from that of the three major neo-classical painters, but there are points where they intersect and all five of them have in common the fact that human figures, dressed or undressed, are essential elements in their paintings. Their 'pure' landscapes, without figures, are almost always tedious, and Leighton's landscapes are boring to an almost unbelievable degree considering his great technical gifts.

Burne-Jones is one of the most interesting and complex of nineteenth-century painters. Outwardly he was ordinary enough, except for the odd fashion of wearing his beard in two long streamers down the side of his face. Born in 1833 at 11 Bennett's Hill in the heart of Birmingham, his father was a wood-carver and gilder, with a shed at the back of the house. A quiet gentle man, he had been widowed twice; there were only a few books in the house, but those were poetry, and the young boy early got into the habit of retreating into a dream world.

Education at King Edward's Grammar School, Birmingham, was a rough reminder of reality; he had a few drawing lessons there, and was forever covering

Edward Burne-Jones established a new kind of nude, small-breasted and narrow-hipped. In this study for *The Three Graces* in black and red chalk on brown paper it is clear that he selected his models with these attributes.

sheets of paper with lightning sketches. There was no thought of his being an artist, and his serious thoughts were turning to the Church. A visit to the Cistercian monastery in Charnwood Forest impressed him deeply, and he involved himself in theology. In 1853 Burne-Jones went up to Oxford, to Exeter College, meeting William Morris (1834–96), who was to prove a lifelong friend and powerful influence, and who turned Burne-Jone's attention away from religion to all that was mediaeval.

Oxford overwhelmed Burne-Jones. It was 'a glorious place . . . godlike . . . Heaven to live and die here'. Although his father was not rich, Burne-Jones ran up the usual undergraduate bills, especially on drink—Madeira, claret, and particularly champagne. Unfortunately Oxford began to disappoint. Everyone seemed uninspired, except Morris and his circle, who formed a romantic movement of their own, with readings from Tennyson, who was finding the Middle Ages in his own best-selling way.

Morris was rich, and founded and edited *The Oxford and Cambridge Magazine*. He had begun to write an odd sort of poetry. 'Well, if this is poetry', he commented, 'it is very easy to write.' Burne-Jones had come across the work of Dante Gabriel Rossetti (1828–82), rich in mediaeval allusions, and became a hero-worshipper. In 1856 he met Rossetti at the Working Men's College then in Great Ormond Street, where Rossetti lectured to the improved working class. A dominating life-intoxicated poet and painter, Rossetti captivated the impressionable Burne-Jones, told him there was no question of his going back to Oxford and that he was destined to be a painter. He referred to Burne-Jones in a letter as 'a certain youthful Jones . . . one of the nicest young fellows in Dreamland'.

Although only five years older than Burne-Jones, Rossetti had a wealth of experience of life behind him. Under his influence, Burne-Jones saw London as a magic place where 'it was always morning and the air sweet and full of bells'. As always, he would retreat when reality impinged on him. Rossetti found Morris and Burne-Jones rooms at 17 Red Lion Square, London, so that he could continue to rivet them with his spell.

A scheme arose to decorate the Oxford Union, where there was space 'hungry to be filled with pictures', as Burne-Jones wrote. He was one of the artists, self-taught with some off-the-cuff instruction from Rossetti. Another was Val Prinsep, later to be a staunch and orthodox Royal Academician: 'What fun we had in that Union! What jokes! What roars of laughter,' wrote Prinsep in later years. The spirit of the Oxford Union community painting spread to Red Lion Square and the happy Bohemianism of the Rossetti circle. It did not last long; they all married, and marriage was inimical to their kind of fun.

William Morris became involved in recreating the Middle Ages, with what Rossetti described wittily as 'intensely medieval furniture, like incubi and succubi', incomparably uncomfortable and carved without knowledge of the original kind of furniture, which above all was functional. Rapture with the past led Morris into socialism and dreams of an Arcadia where gaunt Victorian factories would be replaced by craft workshops, with every man being creator and vendor, consumed with joy. Burne-Jones's mediaevalism led in the opposite direction, and he was supported by his wife, anxious to shield her husband from life.

Uncertain yet of his role, Burne-Jones did designs for a variety of projects—

Cupid's Hunting Ground by Burne-Jones shows his unusual
compositional schemes and his particular brand of fantasy,
and also his talent for desexualizing his men and women.

Burne-Jones's study for *The Mirror of Venus* was painted
about 1868, and demonstrates his painting techniques. In his
pencil and chalk sketches he is far more delicate and precise.

'marvels of finish and imaginative detail' said Rossetti. He became fascinated with
stained glass, and windows executed from his cartoons are to be found all over
England. He made exquisite pen-and-ink drawings on vellum, and began painting,
in both water-colours and oils, beginning to throw off the influence of Rossetti and
finding his own style.

He worked hard and was immensely patient, often having several large
paintings in progress at the same time. The Royal Academy he held in scorn, with
their 'silly unmeaning subjects and those of a more questionable character'. It was
clear that he saw through the open eroticism of the neo-classical artists, but he did
not disdain the nude, and always made delicate pencil sketches of the naked figures
that he later transferred to canvas, clothed.

To give some examples of the lapse in time between the start of a picture and its
completion, *The Wheel of Fortune* was designed in 1871, started in 1877, and not
finished until 1881; a series called *The Briar Rose* was initiated in 1869 but the
finished pictures were not exhibited until 1890. This system had drawbacks, for
delay in finishing a picture resulted in a delay in payment, and when he was paid
before completion he suffered agonies of remorse. His subjects are often strange
and unusual, though some of the stock themes appear, as in the *Mirror of Venus*, a
Pygmalion series, and paintings on the Perseus legend, a subject no artist who
painted the nude could resist.

For many years Burne-Jones was little known. Even his stained glass went
under the name of William Morris, who actually made it. Swinburne dedicated his

Edward Burne-Jones worked in a variety of styles, and was often accused of mannerism and 'preciousness'. *The Depths of the Sea* (1886) was the only picture Burne-Jones exhibited at the Royal Academy and has an unlikely touch of grim humour about it. The mermaid is dragging a man to her cave at the bottom of the ocean without thinking or caring that what is sport to her means death to him.

Sir Joseph Noel Paton (1821–1901) was a painter of subject
pictures, Queen's Limner (artist) for Scotland, book
illustrator and poet. By putting wings on a nude and calling
her a fairy he succeeded in deflecting criticism, and *The
Fairy Queen* is typical of his output in this genre, simpering
but charming.

Poems and Ballads to him in 1867, and the literary world wondered who this man Burne-Jones was, but until 1877 he had only one regular patron, William Graham of Grosvenor Place, well known as a discerning collector of Pre-Raphaelite and early Italian pictures.

The opening of the Grosvenor Gallery in 1877 gave Burne-Jones a perfect showplace for his work. Although the gallery was seen as a deliberate rival to the Royal Academy, many Academicians, including Leighton, exhibited there. Burne-Jones, despite his air of other-worldliness, was an endearing figure with a quaint quirky humour and an altogether Victorian fondness for the pun. Leighton liked him, and it was he who nominated Burne-Jones (without his knowledge) for election to the Royal Academy. As an Associate Burne-Jones exhibited *The Depths of the Sea* in 1886, a strange and beautiful picture in which a mermaid with a most eerie expression is carrying down to the bottom of the sea a naked young man who she has inadvertently drowned in the fury of her love.

In 1886 another event happened to put Burne-Jones even more firmly on the map. His patron William Graham died, and his collection was thrown on to the market. The prices obtained for the Burne-Jones paintings startled everyone, and put him in the same class as Leighton, if not Millais. In the early 1860s Burne-Jones water-colours were selling at between £21 and £44; in 1886 his *Chant d'Amour* made £3,307 10s. His reputation increased as the years went by, and he was a name to reckon with well into the twentieth century, when Leighton and Alma-Tadema were regarded as boring hacks. Indeed, Burne-Jones's star did not begin to flicker until the 1920s.

Having had no systematic art instruction, and thus having avoided being in some way moulded by a strong teacher, Burne-Jones has a lengthy stock of mannerisms, which led to him being accused of affectation, of deliberate imitation of early Italian painting and of indifference to realism. His fondness for symbolism was ridiculed as the aberration of a warped mind. Stylistically he was very varied, and he changed his colour schemes from one picture to another, at one time preferring a bright glowing palette, and others a subdued tonality, seemingly without reference to the subject. His colouring could be rich and succulent, or it could be coarse. He had an affection for sickly greens, a fashionable colour at the Grosvenor Gallery, which favoured the more *avant-garde* artists. The Gallery became identified with the new-fangled aesthetic movement and an easy target for satire.

> A greenery-yallery, Grosvenor Gallery,
> Foot-in-the-grave young man!

This was a reference to the ghastly pallor in the faces of the characters in the art of Burne-Jones and his associates, and also a comment on the painters themselves, who looked as though they were on the point of dying. Many of them consciously adopted this as a pose but it was often more than a pose, the result of drink, drugs and tuberculosis, and many artists of the time died young.

Although Burne-Jones used themes commonplace among the Royal Academicians, he did discover his own, from mediaeval England and Arthurian

Night and *Morning* by F. A. Haviland are decorative panels
clearly influenced by Burne-Jones, as well as by *art nouveau*
graphics. Burne-Jones continued to exert a spell long after
his death—well into the 1920s when Victorian painting was
generally considered dead and buried.

legend. One of the basic differences between Burne-Jones and the Academicians of the Leighton and Alma-Tadema persuasion is that, whereas they reconstituted ancient times, paying due regard to its architecture, Burne-Jones evoked them and lived in them. (His mental state was in consequence a constant worry to his wife who considered that her husband was liable completely to lose touch with reality.)

Burne-Jones made many hundreds of sketches of the nude; poses were drawn over and over again until he felt that he had got the right one. The qualities he sought in his models were neither the bosomy nor the chic, and in his male studies too there is sometimes a reluctance to be specific about the genitals, leaving them a vague blur. He was, however, an excellent draughtsman, and this shows more clearly in the sketches than the finished paintings. His caricatures, when he returned from his dream world into fashionable society, are witty and deft.

When turning his sketches into finished art-work he frequently desexualized his figures, until the distinction between male and female is almost lost, and we see rather distasteful hermaphrodites. At times, though, he could paint sensual and erotic nudes, as for example in his single Royal Academy picture *The Depths of the Sea* and in *The March Marigold*, where he uses transparent drapery to trace the line of the leg. Had he not been averse to the Royal Academy and painting by formula he might have adopted its ethos, but after his one exhibit there he withdrew from it, preferring the Grosvenor and, later, the New Gallery.

The year of the opening of the Grosvenor Gallery (1877) was the year when Ruskin launched his celebrated attack on Whistler ('I have seen, and heard, much of cockney impudence before now; but never expected to hear a coxcomb ask two hundred guineas for flinging a pot of paint in the public's face.'). After much heart-searching, Burne-Jones, originally lined up with Whistler and 'art for art's sake', went over to Ruskin, an experience which reinforced his aversion to real life.

The ambiguity and the curious overtones in the work of Burne-Jones strongly influenced up and coming Continental artists, especially in France and Germany, and he regularly exhibited in Paris, both at the official Salon and at independent galleries. In 1904 an exhibition of Burne-Jones's drawings in Barcelona caught the eye of the young Picasso, who was most impressed by them.

It would not be too much to say that there is a strong element of suppressed sexuality in much of the work of Burne-Jones, and it was this that gave it an intense interest to young painters of subsequent generations. The kind of work which Burne-Jones did, where the medium demanded simplification and stylization—as in book illustration, particularly the work he did for William Morris—caused a tug-of-war between content and execution which often gave piquancy to his work. In 1865, for example, Morris and Burne-Jones had conceived the idea of an illustrated edition of Morris's *Earthly Paradise*. The project was not carried out, but Burne-Jones did forty-four illustrations to one section, *Cupid and Psyche*, which provide insight into not only the way Burne-Jones worked but his motivations and private thoughts on the matter.

Although forever an outsider and unmotivated by success, Burne-Jones was made a baronet in 1894. He died in 1898, an example of an artist who could thrive without the backing of the Royal Academy, and someone who exerted a powerful influence both in Britain and abroad largely because of accidental features in his work, not seen by the artist himself or his close associates.

II

WATTS AND DORÉ - THE GRAND GESTURE

If Leighton could throw timid Academicians into a tremble by exhibiting his versions of Venus, if Alma-Tadema affronted Victorian matriarchs with equally Victorian daughters in a state of undress, and if Poynter had his naked women draped suggestively by sea-shore or at the openings of caves, everyone felt safe with George Frederick Watts, whose nudes discouraged more men than they encouraged.

Watts was the Grand Old Man of Victorian painting, and his somewhat eccentric life style did nothing to mar the image, at which he worked diligently. Born in 1817, the son of a piano-maker in Marylebone who tuned pianos and gave music lessons to supplement a meagre income from his trade, there was an early indication that he would never want for food and shelter. He had an easy charm that turned acquaintances into patrons, and patrons into universal providers.

As a boy, he was let loose in the studio of the sculptor William Behnes (Sculptor in Ordinary to Her Majesty) (1795–1864), watching him make statues and produce portrait medallions. Watts imbibed knowledge apparently through the pores of the skin, never had any skilled tuition, picking up what he wanted as he went along. He became friends with a Blackheath schoolmaster who, under the name of Nicholas Felix, played professional cricket (his book *Felix on the Bat* is the supreme classic of cricketing literature). In return for schooling in music and languages, Watts did seven lithographs of the positions in cricket, demonstrating his skill in drawing.

Constantine Ionides, the rich Greek merchant and art-patron, befriended Watts, and in 1843 the State became Watts's patron when his design *Caractacus Led in Triumph Through the Streets of Rome* won a £300 prize in a competition to find suitable paintings to adorn the new Houses of Parliament. With this money he decided to go to Italy, and there he met Lord Holland, British Minister at Florence, was invited to lunch and then to stay, which he did for several years, before returning to London in 1847. There he again won an official prize, this time of £500. 'A great fellow or I am much mistaken,' said Ruskin, and Watts agreed.

He fell in with the Prinsep family, for whom Watts had found a house to let on the estate of Lord Holland—Little Holland House, two miles from Hyde Park, and not at all little but rambling and romantic. 'He came to stay three days', Mrs Prinsep said later, 'and he stayed thirty years.' Little Holland House was the centre of an artistic suburb long before the creation of the present postal district, Holland Park, and Watts was supplied with ample subject matter for his excellent and penetrating portraits. It was a splendid situation for a recluse often in a poor state of health—though Watts outlived most of his famous contemporaries.

In a moment of self-indulgence Watts married a teenage girl, who unfortunately happened to be lively, and unwilling to be a daughter-surrogate. She was, in fact, Ellen Terry, the actress, and the marriage was quickly brought to an amicable end without complications, leaving Watts free to continue his mission. This was to uplift art single-handed, to eradicate all that was frivolous and to paint vast allegorical and symbolical pictures. Favourites were love, in the most rarefied sense, justice, and hope. He held a grand Victorian vision of painting ideas and not common subjects, though he did these when he was under par. Two of these unWatts-like pictures are *Found Drowned* and *Under a Dry Arch*, though in their own way these are moral lessons of the kind many of his contemporaries liked to paint.

'I want to make art the servant of religion,' he wrote. 'I want to assert for art a yet higher place than it has hitherto had.' From other artists this manifesto would have sounded prim and egotistical, but from Watts it was accepted. 'I am a thinker', he proclaimed, 'who happens to use a brush instead of a pen.' His thinking was hardly deep. In his symbolical picture *Love and Life* the aim was to show that love ('by which, of course, I mean not physical passion, but altruism, tenderness') leads man to the higher life.

In depicting the idea of love, whether or not it is altruistic and tender, or physical, it is difficult, if not impossible, to avoid personalizing love as a naked man or woman, a Cupid or a Venus. Watts certainly had no objection to the depiction of naked women. The ideal, he defined, was 'that form which most emphasizes human characteristics furthest removed from suggestions of the inferior creatures—a principle so well understood and acted upon by the great Greek artists'.

He had a high opinion of contemporary womanhood—'The modern young lady is often of splendid growth and form such as probably the ancient Greek never saw.' He maintained that their figures were being ruined by the dictates of fashion, and was a member of the Anti-Tight-Lacing Society, which hated the corset to a point not far short of obsession.

The aim of the corset was the wasp-waist, a phenomenon which focused attention on the breasts and the hips. Not surprisingly, the Anti-Tight-Lacing Society contained members who deprecated developed sexual characteristics as well as those who honestly thought that tight lacing was a cause of ill-health, as indeed it was. The invention of the metal eyelet meant that great pressure could be applied on the cloth and whalebone corset, and husbands and servants were recruited to pull the strings of the corset tight while the unfortunate wearer held on to a suitable object, such as a bedpost. Tight lacing could cut the liver nearly in two, and was a frequent cause of fainting.

It would be charitable to assign to Watts the view that tight lacing was medically damaging, but it is more likely that he objected aesthetically. He was thoroughly in tune with advanced thinking, and the young women of the period who believed in emancipation and modernity rejected tight lacing and wore loose or functional clothing, often in the Greek style, or what was construed as the Greek style.

He was never tired of framing his opinions. 'My intention has not been so much to paint pictures that charm the eye, as to suggest great thoughts that will appeal to the imagination and the heart, and kindle all that is best and noblest in humanity.' The main object of the painter should be 'demanding noble aspirations, condemning in the most trenchant manner prevalent vices, and warning in deep tones against lapses from morals and duties'. From other artists this would have seemed pious platitude, but Watts meant every word. Critics warmed to him. It was 'the rare combination of supreme handicraft with a great imaginative intellect which secured to Watts his undisputed place in the public estimation of his day'. The general public were told that this was great art, and they believed it, believing even the most committed of supporters who equated Watts with Titian. It did not matter that the symbolism had to be explained before the picture was understood. A female figure bending blindfolded on the earthly globe sounding the sole remaining string on her lyre while a solitary star shines from the heavens was utterly mysterious until the title of the picture was read—*Hope*. Sometimes the mystery

Fata Morgana by G. F. Watts (1817–1902) shows a flirtation with the mediaeval period, and the nude is a good deal more luscious than is usual with this most uneven of painters. It was in the collection of the gold-mine tycoon, George McCulloch. Painted in 1865, it was exhibited at the Royal Academy in 1870.

Dawn was painted by Watts in 1887 when every picture he
painted had to have a symbolic or profoundly mysterious
title. His indifference to textures is evident by the unpleasant
configuration of the drapery, though the nude is done well
enough.

remained, but the public was assured that they were looking at great art and did not mind.

Watts could be a strong and trenchant artist. *The Minotaur*, exhibited in 1896, has a power and intensity that would be acceptable among the twentieth-century Surrealists, and many of his subjects have the kind of ambivalence favoured by Poynter, who, however, took care to include succulent nudes. Watts's nudes are never succulent, and in *Love and Life* for example, the nude is a barely formed adolescent girl, hipless with small buttocks and gawky legs.

Love and Life was one of Watts's most popular pictures, and he did several versions of it; one of them was exhibited in 1885, one of them was owned by the Metropolitan Museum, New York, and another was in the Louvre, where it no doubt impressed earnest Frenchmen faced with the open salaciousness of so much work in the Paris Salon. The *Love and Life* nude was described by Watts as 'an emblem of the fragile quality in humanity, at once its weakness and its strength'. It is a strange product from a man who at an early age haunted the British Museum and who later declared that all the art he knew was learnt staring at the Elgin Marbles. The hypnotic power of the Elgin Marbles is never better displayed than in its complicated effect on the art of Watts.

Misty allegory with high moral overtones could not be attacked. Watts was made an Associate of the Royal Academy in 1867 and, probably realizing that it was being tardy, the council made him a full Member in the same year. He often exhibited at the Grosvenor Gallery and subsequently at the New Gallery, and a Watts painting was part of the visual landscape of the art world, for better or for worse. One of his closest friends was Leighton, for whom Watts was something of a trial, as man and artist. The beautiful finish of the most accomplished academic painters was alien to Watts, and Leighton had often to request Watts to make his Royal Academy pictures at least presentable, even if it meant last-minute alterations on the spot. Watts's colour-sense too was often abysmal, and Leighton used to beseech him to dab a bit of this or that colour on to lend some harmony.

Arrogant in his views, set in his ways, bolstered up by the prestige he enjoyed as a man who set out great abstract ideas in paint, Watts had a technique that his friends called individual, straightforward and simple. It meant leaving off when he felt that he had done enough. His later works give the impression of a dislike of paint. The rough coarse canvas he liked was often left blank, or so thinly covered that the texture shows through. He laid on pure colours without mixing them on the palette (as did the Impressionists, with a totally different effect); he ignored detail, and he did not like his objects to have firm outlines, preferring to see them melt into the background. Flesh and foliage have the same sort of appearance.

Despite his shortcomings, Watts had a powerful influence, and set painters off scurrying into allegory and pretentiousness. High motives, it was felt, were more important than technique, and those who took Watts at his own valuation, rather than as a repressed man anxious to take the sex out of the human figure, went along with this trend.

One of the men Watts admired to excess was Cecil Rhodes, who was seen to have possessed—in Watts's view—his own practical idealism. In later life Watts went into sculpture, and his man on a horse entitled *Physical Energy*, originally intended for the Embankment, was set among the Matoppo Hills in Africa, to the

The subject of Doré's *The Tortured Lovers* comes from Dante,
and illustrates his love of sinuous modelling, preferably
coupled with heavy drama. Unlike many painters, Doré was
well served by his engravers.

astonishment of the natives. A copy was set up in Kensington Gardens. He was nearly seventy when he married again, and he and his wife set up an art pottery in Compton.

As an antidote to the Victorian erotic nude, Watts has few equals, and he was needed to counter the dangerous view that naked women could be sexually arousing. Certainly he was no fraud and, unusual for painters in the public eye, he turned down a baronetcy, accepting the Order of Merit from King Edward VII instead. King Edward too liked grand gestures, though it is doubtful if Watts's women appealed to him personally.

A painter who shared Watts's appetite for the grand style was Gustave Doré, who enjoyed a phenomenal success with his great canvases, which he showed at his own gallery in New Bond Street. As with Watts, there was nothing subtle about Doré. He received his inspiration from literature, and whatever he illustrated he interpreted in his own manner, which involved struggling and writhing naked men and women, which he fitted into scenes from Tennyson, Dante or the Bible.

His technical skill and his mastery of theatrical effects were seen at their best in his engravings, of which he did tens of thousands. His paintings, most of which have passed out of sight, look as though they were painted with sump oil, but this did not matter, for it was the message and not the medium that was important. The message was simple; the French and English public liked globe-breasted long-legged women preferably in abandoned postures, and he would provide them, with no pretence of spirituality or refinement.

Between 1850 and 1870 he earned from his art £280,000. One of his supporters, who edited a vast book of Doré engravings, was Edmund Ollier, who wrote about the artist's women's 'animal luxury', and admitted that when Doré turns to 'the gentleness and grace of the female character in its perfection of physical culture and moral loveliness . . . he becomes tame or uncouth'.

Doré threw his naked women at the viewer in a way rare among English painters, and he had his reward not only in cash but in a mesmerized response. In 1872 the Rev. Francis Kilvert did his annual rounds of the London galleries, and on his agenda was Doré's gallery:

There was a new picture there, an Andromeda, a handsome graceful girl life size, well painted, the flesh tints very natural. The slender girlish form is bowed and shrinking from the monster, the white feet are washed by the lap of the green waves, the manacled hands and wrists are straining at the chain and that rich brown hair is blown wildly forward from the bowed back and beautiful shoulders across the horror-stricken face.

Thoroughly unnerved, Kilvert took the train back to his flock in Herefordshire, hoping to find an Andromeda there whom he could rescue, and no doubt being disappointed. Art and life did not always correspond.

Doré was one of art's men with a megaphone, within an ace of being pornographic, but no one can deny his immense power as an illustrator. He is best known today as the illustrator of Blanchard Jerrold's *London*, and his magnificent drawings of London low-life have the force of a documentary.

Doré's *The Deluge* brings together two of his favourite
subjects—a damsel in distress and twisting bodies.
Considering the Victorians' delight in melodrama, it is not
surprising that the exhibitions of his work at his own gallery
in New Bond Street were enormously popular.

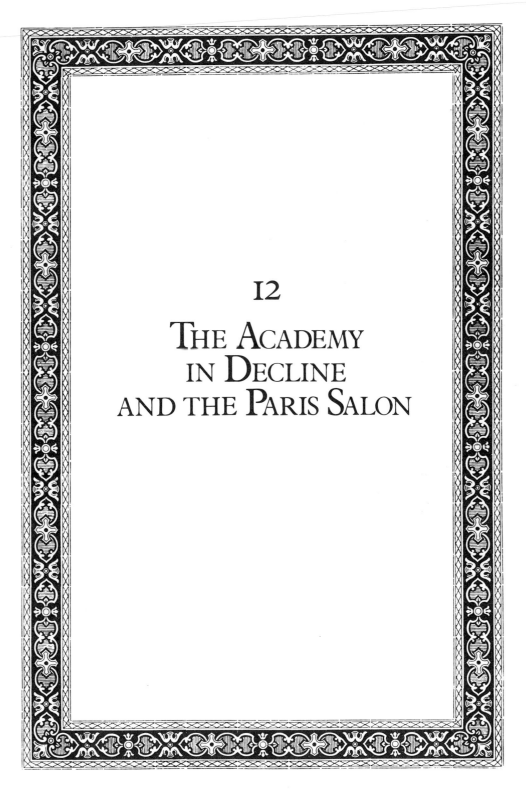

12

THE ACADEMY
IN DECLINE
AND THE PARIS SALON

During the Presidencies of Leighton and Poynter the supply of nude subjects to the Royal Academy exhibitions did not falter and, indeed, the changing climate of the times meant that there was no objection from the critics when the topics became saucier and the sexual undertones became overtones. Throughout the age a good deal of licence had been permitted to artists in their day-to-day lives. Simeon Solomon, a painter of vague and visionary subjects, was an unashamed homosexual; Rossetti was a roisterous and uninhibited fornicator. But it happened that men who were sexually extrovert did not have the need to express their thoughts on naked women in paint.

The painters of the most thought-stimulating pictures were largely quiet and respectable men (and women) who went about their everyday lives in relative obscurity, enjoying brief moments of glory when their Royal Academy pictures were referred to by the critics in terms which were rarely caustic. The office of critic since the disappearance of Ruskin from the scene was rather one of commentator, and when there were critics with a jaundiced set of values (such as Tom Taylor and Harry Quilter) their energies were directed at what they considered advanced and impertinent art, such as that by Whistler. Occasionally they scolded the French artists who exhibited at the Salon for their excesses, but usually in moderation. There was no point in upsetting the art market by pursuing a witch-hunt and, more to the point, the proprietors of the newspapers were even less anxious for the sour note of genuine antipathy.

There are many opinions about the exact date when Victorian prudery began to weaken, and the muffler of respectability was lifted. There were certainly a large number of contributive factors which reduced the power of the class which held that it had a God-given right to exercise a censorship on morals—the middle class, and especially middle-class women. An important aspect was the increasing self-confidence of the working classes, largely literate since the coming of compulsory education in 1870, and resenting the crippling code of morals laid down for them to follow. Cheap newspapers pulled no punches in their reporting, and the *News of the World* and *Reynold's News* found that there was increased circulation to be found in the detailed accounts of salacious court cases. The reporting of divorce cases was carried out in full until pressure was put on the newspapers to curb their enthusiasm. There was a great variety of semi-underground newspapers, and whereas societies for the suppression of vice had flourished in the 1860s and 1870s they were now poorly supported and were in flustered disarray.

At one time, anything that savoured of the sexual was attacked and subjugated to protect innocent womankind. With the growing agitation for women's rights, the first cries of the Suffragette movement and the demand for women to operate the new typewriters, the cries for protection from the facts of life seemed to come from a wilderness. Freedom for women had its effect on the art world; more young girls were going to art schools, and although there were some schools which kept them out of the life class there were far more where male and female students mixed on equal footing.

Opposite Many artists were influenced by the drama of Doré and the symbolism of Watts and, although Solomon J. Solomon (1860–1927) is best known as a portrait and subject painter, his *Sacred and Profane Love* contains many echoes of his two famous elders.

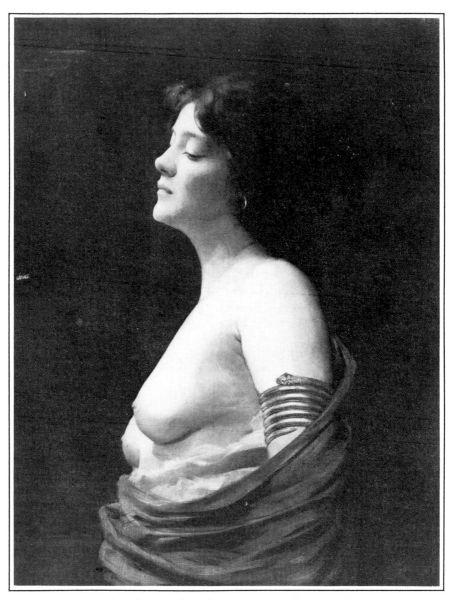

Above Vesta by Isaac Snowman, painted in 1895 and
exhibited at the Royal Academy in 1896. Vesta was the
chaste goddess who presided over the family. Despite the
title, this is a straightforward erotic picture in the
photographic-realistic style.

Opposite H. Granville Fell is mainly known as an illustrator
for popular magazines, but his sense of design and colour
schemes have great charm. *Autumn* was published in *The
Pall Mall Magazine* in 1899, when nude figures in the
illustrated magazines were no longer greeted with horror.

Victorianism did not end overnight, and those who thought that a golden age had arrived with everyone free to do what they wanted when they wanted received a rude shock when Oscar Wilde was sent to prison for two years for homosexuality. Newspaper editors could get away with almost anything, but respectable publishers found themselves attacked and sometimes prosecuted when they ventured into areas which had been forbidden to them and which they had fondly imagined had become open ground. Books and pamphlets on birth control continued to be banned, as did most books on sex, though nude photographs printed for the benefit of artists somehow found their way on to the market.

Publishers envied the Royal Academy artists who were free to exhibit nude paintings which in another medium or another location would get them arrested. It was often difficult to understand why this was, and how Academicians could escape prosecution. In 1892 came a fascinating test case, in which the immunity of painters of the nude was put on trial.

Edward Cox was a solicitor's clerk, who had spent forty years in one employment, and was now out of work. While walking down the Strand he was given a hand bill which invited spectators to visit a certain address and see a picture called *The World's Desire*, the subject of which was 'naked and not ashamed'. Cox responded to the invitation and went to see the picture. He considered it 'obscene, lewd, wicked, filthy and indecent'. He took action against the artist, Rudolf Blind, and the matter was brought to the magistrate's court at Bow Street.

Blind's counsel, Mr Rose-Innes, realized that he was involved not with some trivial matter but something of consequence. He asked for a three-week adjournment while he could consult eminent artists, and this was granted, provided that the picture remained in the confines of the court. Rose-Innes commented that if Blind's picture was declared obscene, 'half of those in the National Gallery would come under a similar ban'.

News of the action spread like wild-fire, and when the case reopened the public galleries were full of the most eminent artists of the day. The picture was brought out. It showed Eros, the god of love, and Beauty, the world's desire, together with cherubs symbolizing mirth, merriment, and gaiety, and there were also figures demonstrating the various stages of mankind. The question was not whether the picture was beautiful (of which there was 'no question', whatever that may have meant) but whether it was obscene, under Lord Campbell's Act, 20 & 21 Vict. Sect

Opposite above The Salon was the Paris equivalent of the Royal Academy, but a considerable amount of licence was allowed the artists, who sometimes overstepped the line into bad taste. *La Fin des Sirènes* by the little-known artist, A. La Lyre, was a typical exhibit.

Opposite below The French artists who exhibited at the Salon were rarely obliged to pretend that they were painting mythological pictures. *Baigneuses* is clearly a study of contemporary Parisian *grisettes*, and the fashionable Japanese parasol dates it firmly in the 1890s. Of course, great artists such as Degas and Toulouse-Lautrec had established a kind of realism in their nudes that minor artists such as Paul Tillier could not touch.

1, more commonly known as the Obscene Publications Act of 1857, which made it a misdemeanour to exhibit a work which was obscene.

Edward Cox was interrogated, and admitted that he knew nothing about art, had never been to the Royal Academy and had never been abroad, though what that had to do with the matter was not made clear. Asked whether there were any boys or girls looking at the picture, he said that he thought not. An engineer and former journalist, John de Morgan, was also handed a bill in the Strand, but he made no contributions to the case.

Blind's counsel brought as witness the eminent painter of Eastern scenes, Frederick Goodall, RA, who maintained that the picture was not obscene. The prosecution did not let it rest there—'This is intended to be a representation of the human figure; would you consider the exhibition of the female figure is obscene?'

Goodall, seemingly perplexed by the argument, answered: 'This is a picture. You never find in nature a perfect form. You have to go to many to find one.' The prosecution persisted. 'I am suggesting to you that this is a representation of the human form.' Goodall responded in the same vein:

The finest works of the old masters are true ideals of the human figure. The exhibition of the human figure itself would, I should say, be obscene.

The prosecution seemed to be trying to make some connection between a real woman and a facsimile of a real woman. It was brought in that there were several pictures of nudes at the Royal Academy that very year, but no one asked whether they were 'representations'. In fact, the bulk of the trial was given over to artists proclaiming that the picture was not obscene. Stacy Marks did not see anything suggestive or improper, a Mr Fellew said that the picture was painted 'in accordance with the conditions of the representation of the nude'—presumably Blind had not made the mistake of depicting pubic hair, which would have made the picture obscene. Fellew went on to make this clear. He did not find 'sufficient realism in it to make it obscene'.

Christie Murray for the defence made a counter-attack on the prejudices and attitudes of people such as Cox. There was, he stated, a 'wilderness of dirt in the minds of the people who saw it as obscene'. Other artists, and an art critic, a Miss Wilson, stood up to defend the picture. The magistrate, Vaughan, dismissed the case, and the Royal Academicians in the public gallery broke into prolonged applause.

This judgment gave a go-ahead to painters of the nude, and also to magazine proprietors. Nude illustrations appeared in the popular magazines such as *Pall Mall Magazine*, often stylized, accompanying short stories or poems, or used as decorative devices for chapter headings or page borders.

Nude statuary was rarely attacked, for it was accepted that sculptors were the inheritors of the ancient Greek tradition and were therefore above reproach. The decorative devices used in *art nouveau*—the fashionable movement which influenced the design of everything from candlesticks to buildings—were also exempt from criticism, and trinket trays, door-plates, cutlery-handles, and light-fittings incorporating nude figures were as free from condemnation as the exhibits of the Great Exhibition in 1851.

Even at a time when the Royal Academy was under siege as
old-fashioned and reactionary, an artist such as Arthur
Hacker (1858–1919) could produce and exhibit a powerful
and suggestive painting such as *And There Was a Great Cry
in Egypt*, shown at the Royal Academy in 1897.

It is interesting to look at the Royal Academy exhibits of 1892, to see what
pictures would have been at risk if the lawsuit against Rudolf Blind had succeeded.
Certainly there would have been a question mark against Frank Dicksee's *Startled* in
which a naked woman and an adolescent girl are proceeding at no great speed from
the banks of a river as a Viking-style barge approaches. Judiciously placed drapery
conceals the woman's private parts. Dicksee (1853–1928) had first shown at the
Royal Academy in 1876, and was a prolific and efficient producer of literary
pictures. George Jacomb-Hood was of the same generation, and for his nude study
of a standing girl he picked the unexceptional title of *Summer*. Jacomb-Hood was
educated at the prestigious Slade School of Art in London and in the studio of the
French artist, Laurens. He was an all-rounder, proficient in black-and-white as well
as colour, and he made a good living as an illustrator for the *Illustrated London News*
and the *Graphic* (an occupation that was hit by the arrival of the half-tone process in
1882, which meant that photographs could be reproduced in newspapers and
magazines). He was also sent out to Greece and India to do on-the-spot work.

Arthur Hacker (1858–1919) was a more considerable artist with a fondness for
symbolic and mystical themes with a decidedly erotic element, who had obtained

his art education at the Royal Academy Schools, and in a Paris studio. His 1892 Royal Academy exhibit was harmless enough, a small-breasted, fully exposed nude called *Syrinx*, but in 1897 he was to create something of a stir with his *And There Was a Great Cry in Egypt*, a Biblical title for a floating lady, representing the destroying angel, against an ill-defined and misty background. In this picture Hacker explored the revealing effect of transparent black drapery.

Even the apologist of the *Magazine of Art* supplement to the Royal Academy Exhibition confessed that it was no more than an average year. Leighton had provided a religious picture, *And the Sea Gave Up the Dead*, mournful and dreary and, although providing a nude of a kind, Poynter was not at his best. There was a reluctant admission that the younger generation of artists were 'imbibing from France the subtler truths of modern execution', but this was coupled with an attack on the Salon, with its 'sameness of conception, of realisation, of execution'. These were just the charges directed against the Royal Academy.

Today the French Salon of the nineteenth century is regarded with an indifference compounded with contempt, and the artists who exhibited there are too often seen as mediocre. They can hardly be said to have practised the same art as Degas, the Impressionists, the Post-Impressionists and Toulouse-Lautrec, but, like the Royal Academicians, the painters of the Salon were providing a product which the public wanted, often with more skill. Although the French middle classes could be as sanctimonious as their brothers and sisters in Britain they were more easily deflated.

The concealed eroticism of British public art was replaced at the Salon by open salaciousness, and the vein of sado-masochism which runs through a significant segment of British art is exploited to the full by the French artists. Leroy's *The Bath* would in Britain have verged on pornography. It was regarded with suspicion by the critic of the *Magazine of Art*, who described it as:

> . . . sufficiently learned to secure its acquisition by the State; the colouration of the principal figure is doubtless admirable, yet the whole picture seems as coolly calculated as its arrangement, and in spite of the skill with which female modesty has been suggested, the work fails of complete success.

Such a long-winded piece of prattle demonstrates the poverty of English art criticism.

J. J. Henner's *Levite of Ephraim and Dead Wife* went further than any Royal Academy exhibit in its thinly disguised necrophilia. A man, his intentions all too apparent, is gazing down at a naked woman prone on a slab.

> Effective and beautiful as it is it is a mere convention as regards true painting of flesh. The picture of a glistening white body lying upon its back is but a variation played by the painter upon his *Dead Christ*.

So declared the *Magazine of Art*.

One of the most typical of French Salon artists was Raphael Collin, and his *Spirit of Contemplation*, shown in the Salon of 1901, left its English critics somewhat breathless.

Every year Henry Scott Tuke (1858–1929) exhibited at the
Royal Academy his inimitable studies of naked boys and
young men. Painters such as Tuke reinforced the suspicion
that at the Royal Academy nothing changed. Although this
particular painting, *The Three Companions*, was exhibited in
1905, it could have taken an unremarked place twenty
years earlier—or twenty years later.

His women are nearly all of a Northern type: tall and straight-limbed, with that peculiar transparence of skin that suggests ice and roses.

Of the picture itself, it showed:

A figure full of grace 'nude yet clothed in thought', audacious yet not startling, challenging yet unconscious of the appeal.

The *Spirit of Contemplation* was, when one has finally broken through the smoke-screen of the critic, a certain B. Kendall, no more than a girlie picture, intended to arouse and excite. Collin 'delights in intricate pose, in abrupt foreshortenings, and difficult perspective'. In other words, Collin liked his women to be writhing and throwing themselves about provocatively.

Collin was sufficiently appreciated to be commissioned to do the décor for the Opéra Comique in 1899, and his ceiling of the Odéon Theatre, Paris, is a cunning reworking of those vast Baroque compositions in which angels and other religious personages float in space. Collin substituted Parisian *grisettes* for angels, and the cavorting male nudes in his Paris ceilings have little of the dignity of the Baroque gods.

In the 1890s exhibitors at the Royal Academy cultivated a similar field. Mythological subjects which would serve as handy pegs to hang group nudes on were relentlessly exploited. The 1893 exhibition was rich in Circes. Circe was the enchantress from Homer, and she could be interpreted as a hag or (in the picture by Hacker) a bewitching naked girl. The valuable point about Circe is that she was a figure being contemplated by men, a subject that appealed to voyeurs (and voyeurism was strong amongst Victorian men—brothels were fitted out with peep-holes so that copulating couples could be watched in secret).

The most tireless exponent of group nudes was H. S. Tuke whose pictures of adolescent boys swimming or lounging about became a regular feature of successive exhibitions. Typical of the all-female groups was *Psyche at the Throne of Venus*, by Henrietta Rae, who was married to another painter of the nude, Ernest Normand. In the same year (1894) Ernest Normand provided a perfect example of the mixed group nude, *An Alien*, in which a group of Arabs are gazing at a white naked girl who has just divested herself of what seems to be a bath towel, and whose intentions are certainly not ambiguous. *An Alien* was a saucy variation on the early Victorian slave-girl theme.

Henrietta Rae is interesting in that she was a successful artist in a sphere dominated by men. Born in 1859, she studied at the well-known art school, Heatherley's, then at the Royal Academy Schools. She first exhibited at the Royal Academy in 1880, and did not miss a year. She was never an Associate, let alone a Member, so she never had a right to put pictures in and her exhibits were selected by the Hanging Committee on their merits. The majority of her pictures are based on

Opposite Typical of the new generation of artists was Byam Shaw, born in 1872 and a contributor to *Comic Cuts*. This page of studies for illustrations to poems by Robert Browning show a distinctive talent and a realistic approach to the nude figure.

mythology, but when she was invited to provide a fresco for the Royal Exchange she tactfully selected the subject of Dick Whittington. Her yearly exhibits at the Royal Academy prove that her brand of racy nudes was acceptable. Her *Psyche at the Throne of Venus* was ostensibly based on passages from William Morris's *The Earthly Paradise*, the same passages that fired Burne-Jones's illustrations done at the request of Morris:

> From her lips unwitting came a moan,
> She felt strong arms about her body thrown.

A popular voyeuristic theme was the sea-maiden, a naked woman being drawn up by fishermen in a net. Sometimes the woman had legs, sometimes a tail (the mermaid variation). Out of water, and sitting on rocks, the sea-maiden could be called a sea-nymph, and B. E. Ward did a fetching one for the 1894 Exhibition. She could also be transmuted into a mythological siren, as by J. Longstaff, who did a huge picture on this topic (126 by 86 inches), incorporating a floating skull to point the message. J. M. Swan's interpretation was more serene, and his looser finish illustrates a trend away from photographic realism.

One of the most captivating of the nymph pictures was *Hylas and the Nymphs* (1897) by J. W. Waterhouse (1849–1917), purchased by the Manchester Art Gallery. Waterhouse, who painted in a stylized and effective manner, not so dissimilar from that of certain Pre-Raphaelite painters, appealed greatly to collectors and museum curators, and three of his paintings were included in the cache that was to form the basis of the Tate Gallery collection.

Waterhouse was distinctive in that instead of vaguely pretty faces which could be interchanged irrespective of the content of the picture he created a certain type of beauty, wholly Victorian and thoroughly of the period. So did John da Costa whose *Idleness* shows a pert nude wearing a head-band. Contemporary props are rare, though a curious example occurs in William Colton's life-size sculpture *The Girdle*.

An artist whose work shows considerable originality is Charles Sims. There is a feyness about his paintings, and a degree of ambiguity, as in his *A Fairy's Wooing*, in which two of the fairies are engaged in an amorous clinch. An unexpected exhibitor was J. Byam Shaw, best-known for his book illustrations, but feeling no doubt that his art education at the Royal Academy Schools obliged him to make a feint at High Art entered a picture called *Whither*, a word apparently taken at random from a dictionary, so little relevance does the picture have to the title.

Wide as the world of mythology was, it could be added to, and Wagnerian legend made an appearance, Venus and Tannhäuser providing an excuse for a naked woman and a naked man on the same canvas (painted by Laurence Koe, a regular exhibitor of nudes or near-nudes). John Collier, always called the Hon. John Collier as aristocratic painters were rare, better known for his precise and admirably painted society scenes, chipped in with *In the Venusberg*.

Twentieth-century nudes are often painted, as nature intended, on a bed, but this was considered too provocative and if it was done, as in Laurence Koe's languorous *Sappho*, the setting had to be remote. In Paris there was licence to use a contemporary subject, as in *A Fairy Dream* in the 1901 Salon, where a naked girl reclines on a bed, her ball-dress thrown off in a heap.

The kind of artist the Royal Academy was *not* keen on—
Aubrey Beardsley, the master of black and white. The Royal
Academy was often criticized for concentrating on oil
paintings to the exclusion of water-colours and graphic
work, but had Beardsley ventured into oils he would still
have had, to say the least, an uphill struggle.

Very few of the painters of the nude of the last twenty years of the nineteenth
century contributed anything new to the form. They painted by formula, choosing
the method that came most easily. There was little heart-searching, a minimum of
experimentation. Many chose the easiest option; painting a girl in water avoided
certain technical problems—if one was good at painting water. A best-selling line
was repeated *ad lib*, and when Ernest Normand found that white naked girls
amongst Arabs was a profitable career he merely rang the changes on personnel and
background.

It seemed that the Royal Academy would never change. When Victoria died and
Edward VII came to the throne, apart from the obligatory portrait or statue of the
dead Queen, nothing happened at the Royal Academy to indicate the change. The

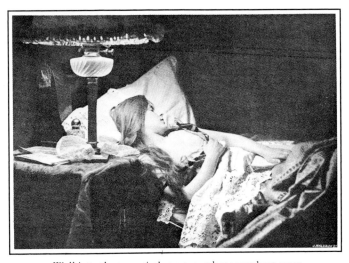

Well into the twentieth century photographers were
influenced by the composition and lighting of paintings,
especially in their nudes and semi-nudes. This study called
Sommeil is by the French photographer C. Puyo.

occasional trenchantly realistic picture at the Academy, epitomized by one of the
first contemporary paintings of social protest, Luke Fildes's *Applicants for
Admission to a Casual Ward* of 1874, threw into greater relief the overall ordinariness
of most offerings.

There were few painters of the nude, with one or two notable exceptions such as
Waterhouse, who in sheer painterly qualities could match the work of Stanhope
Forbes (1857–1947), or in bravura compete with the portraiture of John Singer
Sargent (1856–1925). Nevertheless, although they were artisans rather than artists,
they were not incompetent, and do not deserve to be completely forgotten. Their
paintings often have more interest, if only for unconscious characteristics, than
their neighbours on the august walls, what were known as 'keepsake' pictures,
oozing with sentimentality. Of the profusion of nude children little needs to be said.
They were liked by the kind of people who liked that kind of picture, those to
whom a visit to the Royal Academy was an accepted part of the season, fixed in
amber by *Punch* in 1901:

> Now we can eye with an air supercilious
>   Countrified cousins at function and show;
> Smile while their vigorous bands Piccadilly us
>   In to the pictures or out to the Row.
> Catalogued, ardent, they throng the Academy,
>   Prattle with pleasure or shudder with shocks,
> Startled by nudities Evy or Adamy,
>   Thrilled by the portraits of children in frocks.

Or, indeed, out of frocks. There was no need to question the innocence of naked
children. Of the naked women, especially those staring directly from the canvas with
a come-hither look, there was some doubt.

13
THE NEW LOOK

Royal Academicians naturally thought that the Royal Academy was the centre of British art, but as the century progressed new galleries offered competition. The proprietors of the Grosvenor Gallery and the New Gallery offered a service which the Academy emphatically did not: they went to the artists' studios themselves to discuss likely exhibits. Even distinguished artists had to parcel up their pictures and send them to the Academy if they wanted them considered. In 1886 the Academy received a blow to its self-importance with the formation of the New English Art Club by young painters in revolt. There was consternation in the sacred portals when Whistler was elected President of the Society of British Artists in the same year.

In 1887, the year of Queen Victoria's Jubilee, Whistler sent the Queen some of his etchings. In recognition, Victoria granted the Society a Royal Charter. Whistler invited Monet to send some pictures for the Society's winter exhibition. In 1888 Whistler was forced to resign the Presidency in favour of a safer person, but the winds of change were running through art circles. It was happening in France, too, where French artists were dissatisfied with the Salon and had formed a society of independent artists.

Although there was greater emphasis on social realism and French-inspired muddy landscape, the new London galleries were not revolutionary, and many exhibitors later joined the Royal Academy to become solid members. The mood of the independent galleries encouraged a diluted form of French Impressionism and low-key tonality, exemplified by Sickert (1860–1942). Frivolous nudes were at a discount; if nudes were painted they were in subdued colouring, and had the air of life studies which had somehow been framed and priced. In the early 1900s the New English Art Club lost its vitality and new groupings arose, for the first time offering wall space to modernists, such as the sculptor Epstein (1880–1959). Views varied, and the exponents of one style laid into exponents of another with a will. There were some, such as the influential art critic Roger Fry, who thought that art in the modern state should serve a social function; there were others, such as the followers of the Italian Futurists, who were in love with speed and violence.

It was not a time for nude paintings; the only nudes which created any interest were those done by Epstein to decorate the niches on the new headquarters of the British Medical Association. The first four (of eighteen) were unveiled in 1908 to a chorus of protest. They were indecent, an offence to young womanhood, a symbol of the new art. In 1912 Epstein designed a tomb to Oscar Wilde in the Père Lachaise cemetery in Paris, in which an angel was provided with genitals. The French authorities placed a bronze plaque over them, removed in a night raid by poets and artists.

In 1910 the nude sculpture of Eric Gill aroused controversy. Considering that nude sculpture had enjoyed freedom from censorship throughout the Victorian period even when it was going through its most repressive phases, it is extraordinary that hostility should have been directed against the work of Epstein and Gill, though there is a reason. Both Epstein and Gill eschewed realism of the kind appreciated by the Victorians. They were indifferent to prettiness, and, as Gill wrote in later years, he himself was not interested in the 'superficial delights of fleshly appearance', but in 'the significance of things'.

It was outside conventional art that the possibilities of the nude were exploited, and illustrators stylized and formalized the nude to serve a variety of purposes,

In the 1880s and 1890s there was a revolution in graphic
design and illustration, and one of the leaders was Charles
Ricketts. This illustration from *Hero and Leander* shows his
fondness for distortion and his interpretation of Hero is a
world away from that of G. F. Watts, shown on page 61.

throwing realism out of the window in the cause of novelty. 'Not to be "new" is, in
these days, to be nothing,' wrote H. D. Traill in 1894.

In the 1880s and 1890s there was great adventure in book and magazine
publishing, and short-lived periodicals with small circulations, often privately
printed, encouraged experiment. There was the *Hobby Horse*, the *Pageant*, the *Butterfly*,
the *Dome* and, the most famous of them all, the *Yellow Book*. The publishers Dent and
John Lane were not afraid to extend themselves, offering work to untried artists, such
as Aubrey Beardsley (1872–98). Beardsley, who died young from tuberculosis and
only had six years' working life, tackled the nude with an originality that had rarely
been seen in England. One painter called him 'the representation of all that is
loathsome in art'; to Roger Fry, Beardsley was the 'Fra Angelico of Satanism'. The
Beardsley girl was narrow-eyed, thick-lipped, and ambiguously curved. Beardsley
maintained that he had one aim, to be grotesque, but this was one of his many poses,
cultivated because he knew that it would shock. To the general public, Beardsley
epitomized degeneration and decadence, with the appearance of 'a man from the
Prudential' which overlay, it was alleged, every secret sin that could be named or
imagined—though a friend commented that it was an enigma to him how and where
Beardsley acquired all the knowledge of the dark side of life which his work seemed to
indicate.

Beardsley had been set on his way by Burne-Jones, and it is interesting that he
should have illustrated the story of Cupid and Psyche, as Burne-Jones had done,
though the work he did for William Morris aroused wrath rather than enthusiasm.

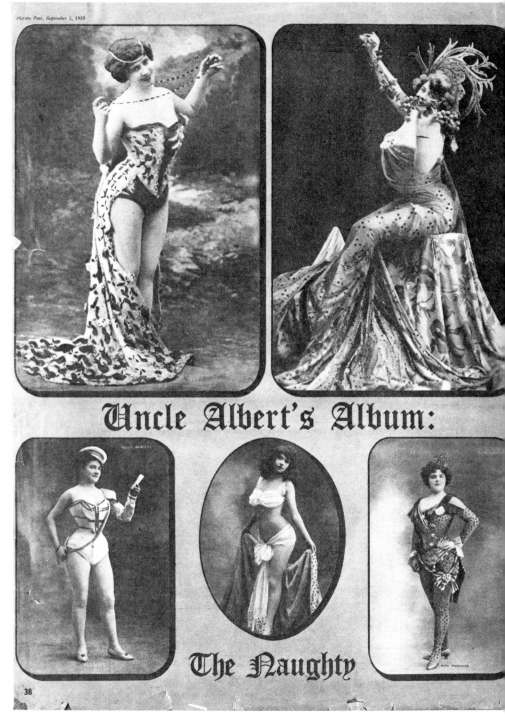

These photographs of ladies, mainly from the *Folies Bergère*, are the kind of images
the Victorian and Edwardian man in the street gloated over. The picture postcard,
introduced early in the present century, provided everyone who had a few coppers
to spend with their own private picture gallery.

Picture Post, September 2, 1939

Our Uncle Albert had a picture album of which he was very proud. The family were not allowed to look at it, but Uncle Albert used to show it to all his old friends whenever they came to visit him. They looked at the pictures and began to talk about the good old days when the 'nineties were naughty, when a music-hall was a music-hall, Paris was Paris and Uncle Albert was a young man. Uncle Albert died last year, and these are some of the pictures we found in his album.

Nineties

39

Morris maintained that Beardsley had perverted his intentions. Some of Beardsley's more sensational drawings were done for Oscar Wilde's *Salome*, and unquestionably he was drawn as if by a magnet to sado-masochistic themes—and if there were none there he provided them, as he did for Pope's *Rape of the Lock*. Beardsley also did some pornographic work, which was lost to sight after his death and has not turned up since.

Conveniently seen as a personification of all that was decadent and depraved, Beardsley was, in fact, a perfectionist and he saw the advantage of using modern methods of reproduction, and that different styles of drawing were needed for half-tone blocks and photogravure. His nudes are completely distinctive; he said that most people are ugly and sensual, and he wanted these qualities to surface in his illustrations.

Beardsley had few followers, but in the art world he had many admirers including Lord Leighton, who bought some early drawings from him. It was thanks to Beardsley's request that Leighton contributed two draped figures to the *Yellow Book*. Leighton also sponsored another young artist, Charles Ricketts, far more versatile, a skilled painter in oils and a sculptor, as well as an illustrator.

Ricketts was born in 1866, and in 1882 was apprenticed to a wood-engraver and met Charles Shannon, with whom he lived for nearly fifty years in perfect harmony. They arranged to follow a programme, Shannon to retire from the world and perfect his painting while Ricketts was to keep them going on illustrative work. Their first co-operative product was *The Dial*, a sumptuous magazine, published in 1889. The design and layout were their own, and acquaintance with Oscar Wilde led to Ricketts designing bindings for him. Success led to the creation of the Vale Press, a pioneer private press. (Ricketts and Shannon lived at the Vale, Chelsea, which had been handed on to them by Whistler who had installed a mistress there, and with whom he was bored.)

Being a free agent, Ricketts could experiment in both typography and illustration, and many of the texts he illustrated demanded the nude. Ricketts's nudes are as emblematic as those by Beardsley, thin and angular, with long streaming hair, a feature which became a cliché of his followers and the *art nouveau* movement in general. He was one of the first to introduce stylized nudes as decoration to the pages of ordinary commercial magazines, conceived as part of the pattern and of no more importance in themselves than a sample of lettering. Ricketts lived on until 1931. He was the dominant partner, though Shannon did some excellent paintings before his mind became unhinged after an accident.

There is nothing of the erotic in Ricketts's work, and the ambiguity between male and female figures echoes a feature that occurs in Burne-Jones. Sometimes the sex of a figure can only be determined by the perfunctory use of an S-shape, denoting a man's genitals. The desexualizing of nudes for the purposes of illustration became commonplace in commercial art-work, for when a more direct representation was demanded photography could be used.

The vigour and invention of the artists of the last fifteen years of the nineteenth century in illustration and graphic design—especially in the poster—and the new directions in art in the Edwardian period—leading to the formation in 1911 of the Camden Town Group which influenced the mainstream of English painting well into the 1950s—what had this to do with the general public? Regrettably, very

In the 1880s and 1890s the decorative possibilities of
pictures began to be appreciated throughout Europe, and
this charming picture, *In the Grotto* by Rudolf Roessler, has
as much care lavished on the rocks and plants as on
the nude figures.

Franz Stuck, born in 1863, was one of the leaders of the Munich *Sezession*, the German and Austrian equivalent of *art nouveau*. Powerful and brooding, *The Sphinx* has something in common with the work of Poynter. The sallow flesh tints are typical of German art of the period and its flavour of decadence.

Opposite Even specialized firms used contemporary art and the stylized nude to appeal to their patrons. The beautifully arranged *art nouveau* typography adds to the appeal of this 1890s' advertisement, directed at the printing trade.

Twilight Thoughts by H. Granville Fell shows the effect of *art nouveau* design on illustration. The trees, the figures and the deliberately lop-sided composition demonstrate the changes that were sweeping through the art of the 1890s and which were to lead in no more than ten years to Cubism and its upheavals.

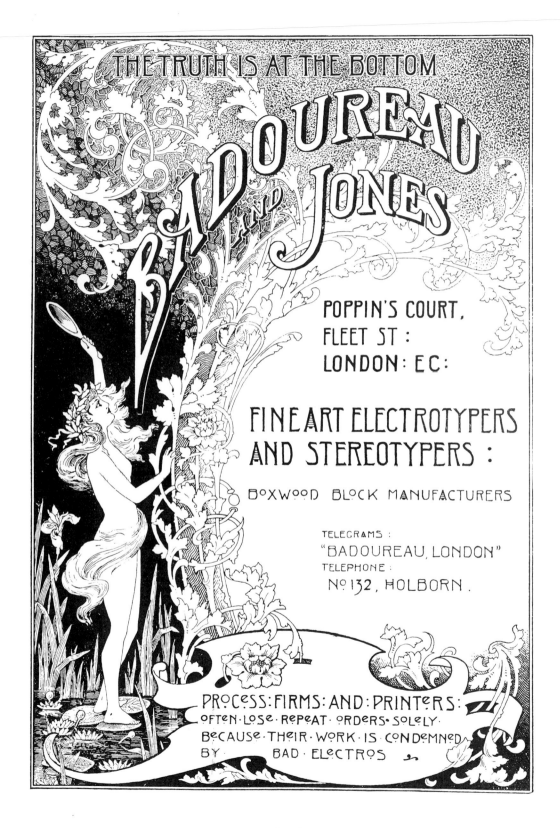

This advertisement from 1897 *Police Gazette* (nothing, of course, to do with the police) shows that despite the winds of change sweeping through the late Victorian period the open sale of quite harmless pin-ups was still not possible.

little. What had this to do with royalty, the upper classes, and the government? Even less. The Royal Academy continued to wield its hypnotic spell. The Exhibition of 1901 merited four long articles totalling 14,000 words in *The Times*. To artists and all those who saw the way art was going this seemed, at the least, to be excessive.

It would be interesting to see how the Royal Academy was affected by the momentous events in art that happened in the first decade of the twentieth century; but the answer is, hardly at all. For connoisseurs of the nude figure, the age of the motor-car, the first aeroplanes, Picasso, the music of Bartok and Stravinsky, might never have happened. Here was the Hon. John Collier with *The Land Baby*, a naked child confronting an equally naked mermaid on a sandy beach, a vague and shimmering picture by Charles Sims, *Ephemera*, and, yet again, *Circe*, by G. A. Storey. Henry S. Tuke contributed his usual picture of naked youths, their bodies carefully arranged to avoid embarrassment. There were more mermaids in *Ulysses and the Sirens* by Herbert Draper, a man who was highly regarded and was given lucrative City commissions, like the adornment of the Draper's Hall (a curious coincidence of names). The most interesting nude picture of the year 1909 was probably *The New Voice* by Byam Shaw, but in Burlington House new voices were not often heard.

As the Edwardian age proceeded, there was new competition for the Royal Academy in the field with which it was so well acquainted—coyness and sauciness. This was the picture postcard. The most risqué were those printed in France, which became known as the home of the dirty postcard. The English manufacturers tried to keep an air of tastefulness and discretion, with flimsily clad actresses and ambiguous tableaux—just as the Royal Academy had tried to do—and, like the Royal Academy, they achieved a good deal of success.

14
METHODS AND MODELS

It is easy to mock the Royal Academy, easier still to forget its many merits. As an institution, with the monarchy and Lord's Cricket Ground, it has survived the vicissitudes of a society and a way of life turned topsy-turvy by the backlash of the Industrial Revolution. No one, for some odd reason, has tried to nationalize it. Each summer the thousands of pictures arrive at its doors to undergo trial by the Hanging Committee, as they did a hundred years ago, though today they arrive by taxi, bicycle and car instead of cab or carriage.

Some of the criticisms that have been directed against it since its inception in the eighteenth century are understandable. It sponsored oil paintings to the neglect of water-colours and it preferred pictures to be about Something rather than Nothing—in other words, the Royal Academy was keen on subject paintings. It has been said that the Royal Academy kept many worthy artists out in the cold, but far more it was the artist's own choice. There was prestige in running against the face of the Academy: two raised fingers at the Establishment.

With the present re-evaluation of Victorian paintings it is gradually being realized that the selection committees could have done a much worse job. Paintings of everyday life by such sterling artists as Mulready (1786–1863) are not only splendid pictures in their own right but are valuable historical documents, and although scenes from the seamy side of life are by no means common, specialists in this field such as Fildes (1844–1927) were not excluded. Nor did it neglect the *plein air* painters—those who stuck their easels out of doors and painted on the spot in the French manner, and two of the greatest painters of this kind, Stanhope Forbes and Frank Bramley (1857–1915), were welcomed. Stanhope Forbes's *The Health of the Bride*, to be seen in the Tate Gallery, is one of the major works of the nineteenth century of any country.

In its willingness to exhibit paintings of the nude, and election to the Presidency of two of the most important painters in this genre, the Royal Academy can be said to have been a bastion of commonsense at a time when pianos were given skirts because legs were indecent and ladies referred to the bosom of the chicken because the word breast could give their friends the vapours. Nude pictures gave offence to the prudish and to churchmen in particular, but the Royal Academy had the courage to face them out.

In 1857 the American novelist Nathaniel Hawthorne was in England, and was confronted by the paintings of Etty:

> The most disagreeable of English painters is Etty, who had a diseased appetite for woman's flesh, and spent his whole life, apparently, in painting them with enormously developed busts. I do not mind nudity in a modest and natural way; but Etty's women really thrust their nudity upon you with malice aforethought...

There were many visitors like Hawthorne, with powerful friends in high places, and it would have been a simple matter for the Royal Academy, had the Members desired, to exert some kind of self-censorship. It is to their eternal credit that this was not done.

If the Academy encouraged subject pictures it also sponsored a quality essential to paint a story so that it is readily understood—technique. Technique can mean many things, but to the Victorians it was basically the means employed to represent a three-dimensional scene on a flat canvas. It was the business of the art school, the art teacher, or the artist who took in pupils to impart the skill to do this.

There were many art schools in Britain, the best known of them being in London. Government-run art schools were a product of the zest for education and improvement, and in the provinces there was overall direction from Kensington, an enlightened place when Poynter was in control. No doubt many provincial art schools, private or official, were excellent, but studying in London or Paris, Rome or Frankfurt, gave additional *cachet* to a young artist keen on making his way in the world.

Most of the art schools in London in the nineteenth century were quite small, and typical of them was one run by Henry Sass in Charlotte Street, who took both boarders and outside pupils. Sass was a very minor artist who occasionally exhibited at the Royal Academy, but was never critically acclaimed, indeed, rather the reverse: 'Mr Sass continues to exhibit a study of something which he persists in calling a head.'

Two of his most famous pupils were Millais (1829–96) and Frith (1819–1909). The regime was boring. Pupils were first set to copy in outline drawings from antique sculpture. This was termed 'drawing from the flat'. When Sass was satisfied that this kind of mechanical copying was being accomplished satisfactorily the pupils were allowed to study the mysteries of light and shade by representing in chalk on white paper a huge white plaster ball set on a pedestal. The shading was done by hatching (a crisscross of single lines); it was a tedious introduction to line-work. The ball was eventually replaced by a bunch of plaster grapes; each grape had its own lights and shadows to tax the pupil. Only when the student had mastered this was he allowed to copy 'the antique'—classical figures and torsos cast in plaster. One student, Jacob Bell, who went on to become a rich chemist and a patron of Landseer and Frith, was so bored with the plaster ball that one day he drew a scaffold with a victim dangling on the end of a rope inside his representation of the ball—and was promptly expelled.

After a student had proved himself in chalk, he was allowed to copy the antique in paint—black and white—and then copy copies of the old masters, which gave many students an intense dislike of them. Students were not expected to express themselves or interpret what they saw; this was regarded as impertinence. The aim of the art school was to train the eye and make the pupil accomplished in drawing, whereupon he might progress to higher things—the Royal Academy Schools, for instance, where admission was dependent on submitted drawings.

The regime at Sass's was paralleled by that at a better-known art school, Heatherley's in Newman Street, and at the very influential Slade School, to which most of the important Edwardian artists went when young. Augustus John (1878–1961) was one of its products, and explained its programme:

The student was first introduced to the Antique Room, which is furnished with numerous casts of late Greek, Graeco-Roman and Italian Renaissance sculpture; no Archaic Greek, no Oriental, no 'Gothic' examples were to be seen. The student was set to draw with a stick of charcoal, a sheet of 'Michelet' paper and a chunk of bread for rubbing out.

A French life school in the 1880s, showing the informal
teaching system available to all who cared to cross the
English Channel. The Royal Academy Schools were often
used as nothing more than stepping-stones to a place in a
French artist's studio.

Like Sass's, the Slade was predominantly a drawing-school; painting was a matter
of tinting a finished drawing as thinly as possible.

Art education generally reflected ordinary education. Slogging was best, no
matter how boring it was, and short-cuts were frowned on. The 'stump' was
anathema to many teachers. The stump is a tight wad of blotting-paper or some
similar substance on which chalk or crayon is scraped. Thus impregnated, the stump
is applied to the paper to give colouring or shading, and thus eliminates cross-
hatching.

When the student got into the Royal Academy Schools he was surprised by the
latitude allowed to him. This was largely due to the laziness and inertia on the
teaching side; no one really cared. Famous artists were nominated Visitors, and
their role was to go to the life class and proffer instruction and advice. A typical
Visitor was Edwin Landseer, who merely turned up with a book, and read.

Small wonder that many young artists found the English art-teaching system
numbing and irrelevant, and found themselves billets in foreign studios, where they
could watch their master at work and do the odd jobs, such as stretching and
priming canvases (priming is sizing a canvas so that it is not absorbent; stretching is

The Model by John S. Sanderson Wells. Despite outsiders'
suspicions, the profession of model was highly respectable.
Italian models were preferred as they were more obedient
and prompt than their English counterparts.

making the canvas rigid by tacking a canvas to a frame and applying wedges from the underside). Favoured pupils might help with the actual painting.

When it comes to painting a picture, there are as many different ways as there are painters, but Lord Leighton's methods illustrate the amount of preparatory work that went into a picture. He first did innumerable thumb-nail sketches or worked out the finished design in his head. He then did sketches from the nude, establishing it in its surroundings, refining it until it was 'squared off' and transferred to canvas. Squaring off is the process in which the pencil or charcoal design is ruled off into squares, making it easier to transfer the design to canvas, which is also squared off. The canvas is usually larger than the paper, so the squares are larger.

If the design is full-size, holes are pricked into the outlines and powdered charcoal is sifted through the holes on to the canvas, revealing a skeleton of the original design, but before the canvas is begun a small oil sketch is made for the colour scheme. This carried out, Leighton painted the figures from life in the nude in a warm monochrome. This was the under-painting. He also drew an exact copy of the nude figures over which detailed drapery studies were later drawn. The draperies were then placed on the nude model, and detailed drawings made. These drawings were then transferred to the nude figure on the canvas, and background and accessories added. A flat colour was then applied to the draperies, fairly thinly so that the modelling of the nude would show through. He then began to put on the colour, preferring stiff colour with very little medium. He kept the surface dead until the later stages, when he would add a coat of medium to liven the painting up.

He was very careful about his colour schemes. Among the colours he regularly used were French ultramarine, French transparent yellow, cadmium yellow and cadmium red, scarlet madder, yellow ochre, burnt white, burnt sienna, indigo, rose madder and madder carmine. Nineteenth-century artists had available to them a large range of colours, including those derived from coal-tar, unknown to earlier painters. These have stood the test of time remarkably well, and many Victorian paintings look as fresh today as they did when they were painted. This was due not only to the pigments they used, but the careful way in which they were applied, often in four or five translucent coats so that at every stage the earlier coats showed through. A painting was built up systematically, often on a gleaming white 'ground' (the all-over colour applied to the primed canvas as the first stage in the picture). The early Victorian buyer in particular liked bright pictures as a reaction to the 'Black Masters' and fairly thin layers on white gave this.

To give sparkle the picture was varnished. This was delayed to shortly before the picture was due for exhibition, and Varnishing Day at the Royal Academy was an institution. On Varnishing Day painters could also make last-minute alterations when something had gone wrong with the colour scheme, and Turner was famous for the way in which he sometimes repainted a picture on Varnishing Day. If Victorian pictures have come down to us somewhat dark and opaque the villain has often been the varnish, which has trapped dirt and blackened in light. Old varnish was one of the reasons why old masters were visualized as essentially dull and dingy, and throughout the nineteenth century there were sporadic attempts to get rid of this old varnish, often by means of chemical fumes.

Many painters, such as Frith, have left few, if any, of their nude sketches. Frith continued to use the nude model however when preparing his large incident-filled paintings, like *Derby Day*, which was the sensation of its year and was roped off to keep away the goggling crowds, though he was a pioneer in the use of photographs, as was Alma-Tadema.

In 1826 Joseph Niepce took the first photograph, a view from his window with an eight hours' exposure. Three years later he went into partnership with Jacques Daguerre, and the success of the daguerreotype led the painter Paul Delaroche to declare that, 'From today, painting is dead.' In 1841 William Fox Talbot patented the calotype process, making prints from a paper negative. Photography was to remain a cumbersome business for many years, but many artists realized the possibilities and either made photographs themselves or collected them. Photography was initially seen as an aid for artists, rather than an art form in itself.

In an exhibition in 1857 O. G. Rejlander, a Swede who lived in England, displayed a large group of nudes and semi-nudes called *Two Ways of Life*. It was made up from more than thirty negatives, for there was no way a photograph could be enlarged. It was a deliberate attempt to imitate High Art, and it caused a sensation, being bought by Queen Victoria and Prince Albert, despite its daringness.

Painting, of course, was not dead. Even with the coming of plate photography, using a coated glass plate, photographs were small and uncoloured, though colour could be applied manually on the print. However, photographs were invaluable for suggesting background to a painting, or in helping out with minor details. Instantaneous photography showed people in motion, very useful to an artist, and by lining up a number of cameras and exposing the lens at tiny intervals it was possible to obtain a series of action photographs. As a result of this the movements of a horse's legs could be analysed, and it was realized that all the animal painters of the past had their facts wrong.

Nude photography, naturally, was very popular, both for private study by artists and for less exemplary reasons. Pornographic photographs were produced by the hundred thousand, sold in plain packets from under the counter in the dirty bookshops of Holywell Street or entrusted to the General Post Office. When the purveyors of pornographic postcards were caught they were sent to prison for long periods; it was a crime which warranted more than a fine.

Painters of the nude relied strongly on good models. Modelling was a respectable occupation, and although the more Bohemian artists might paint their mistresses, the professionals recruited their models with the same care as they did their domestic staff. Many of them preferred Italian models, for English models had a tendency to pose awkwardly, and Italian colonies grew up in the neighbourhood of Kensington. A favourite model was Antonia Cura, painted by Leighton, and used by Burne-Jones to such an extent that she influenced his ideas of beauty in woman and became a kind of prototype. Italian youths and men were highly valued by the painters, especially those who evoked the spirit of ancient Rome and Greece. Relationships between these models and the artists were often regarded with suspicion, for these models sometimes traded on the relationship and expected the painters to sponsor them in other fields—a number of the models themselves wanted to be artists.

Since the invention of photography, artists had been greatly
helped by the camera and nude photographs were widely
available.

A study in chalk by Byam Shaw for *Love's Baubles*. It is
interesting to compare this with similar chalk studies made
by Lord Leighton more than twenty years earlier. There is a
decided change in the faces; these are definitely modern
young ladies. Leighton was more of a perfectionist—even in
a sketch he would not have left one of his nudes
with a club foot.

No female models were permitted in the house of Walter Crane, best known for his children's books (technically 'toy' books), but an occasional painter of luscious nudes, and one of the best known of the male models, Alessandro di Marco, appeared in his picture of Venus as the leading character, to the consternation of Lord Leighton who recognized the model beneath the necessary plumping out. Alma-Tadema also employed Antonia Cura and di Marco, as well as the English model Marion Tatershall, but for his clothed figures he preferred his wife and daughters.

Good models were exchanged between painters—and not necessarily painters. Leighton and Charles Dodgson (Lewis Carroll) shared the charms of the young Connie Gilchrist, Leighton painting her and Charles Dodgson photographing her either in the nude or near-nude. Perhaps Leighton's favourite model was Dorothy Dene, born Pullan; Dorothy Dene was her stage name, for she was an actress as well as a model (largely owing to the influence of Leighton). Leighton passed her on to G. F. Watts, who found her captivating. There was no thought of keeping good things to oneself among the top echelons of painters.

The painters of the Victorian nude reaped a rich reward, and surely no one can say that it was not merited. Perhaps they lived in ivory towers, unaware of the shadow side of Victorian life—the frightful poverty of the poor, the horrors of the northern mill-towns and the exploitation of all who could not stand up for themselves. These painters tell us little of the age they lived in; for that information we go to the painters of genre scenes such as Frith and Augustus Egg, photographs, and the graphic work of cartoonists like Leech and Keene.

With few exceptions, the painters of the nude merely gloried in the beauty of women. That it paid handsomely is the consequence of the combination of two facts—the reverence paid to ancient Greek sculpture and the power of the Royal Academy.

POSTSCRIPT

'Nothing is so chaste as nudity,' wrote George du Maurier in his novel *Trilby*, and as an art student in Paris, where nude models mingled with the pupils as unceremoniously as at a Los Angeles 'love-in', he knew what he was talking about. Du Maurier was more affronted by the coy semi-nudity of fashion, especially evening wear. 'Nothing will ever make me think it right or decent that I should see a lady's armpit flesh-folds when I am speaking to her,' he wrote to his mother in 1862.

Du Maurier was a great satirist of the aesthetic movement, and never tired of poking fun at preciousness, but it was the women of the aesthetic movement who scorned the corset, covered their breasts, kept their natural waists, and adopted a sensible and comely attire. But those who advocated rational dress still accepted that skirts should remain long, even when the wearers were engaged in sports (though knickerbockers were acceptable when cycling).

The emancipation of women started in the last decades of the nineteenth century, accelerated in the Edwardian period and led to the Suffragette movement, but this did not mean a complete shift in attitudes towards dress. The Edwardian lady still bared her breast in the evening, but kept her legs hidden. There was no compromise between dress and undress, no halfway house (as represented in the pin-ups of the 1930s and 1940s—shorts and top, with a bare midriff). The age of the long skirt and the reluctance of women to display their legs lasted until after World War I, except in the fantasy world of the picture postcard, which was a kind of soft porn to young Edwardians.

One great age ended when Victoria died, and the Edwardian period lasted hardly more than a decade. World War I transformed the world and turned morals topsy-turvy. But very little changed at the Royal Academy. Every picture told some kind of a story, and the nudes were still decorous.

Yet even in the 1920s there was a limit to the licence allowed an artist who did not exhibit at the Royal Academy, and who did not follow the official line on the kind of realism 'respectable folk' could well do without. Two policemen raided a gallery in London and seized thirteen paintings. They were 'horrible and filthy productions ... gross, coarse, hideous, unlovely ... and in their nature obscene'. Why were they obscene? The paintings were nudes. The private parts of male and female were 'grossly and unnecessarily developed, with the pubic hair exposed'. The painter was the novelist D. H. Lawrence. A Victorian Royal Academician would not have made such an error of taste!

Opposite A sign of the future—the pin-up. As George du Maurier said, 'Nothing is so chaste as nudity.' The purveyors of saucy postcards knew this and made certain that they did not venture into full-frontal nakedness. The art of disarranging clothes is as subtle as the art of arranging them.

Above The quintessence of Edwardian sauciness was
Raphael Kirchner, whose pin-ups have a knowingness that
anticipates the girlie magazines of half a century on.

Opposite The invention of the picture postcard created great
opportunities for photographers, but it can be seen that the
tradition of providing nudes with classical props, brought
to a fine finish by Lord Leighton and his contemporaries,
was not yet dead.

"A DUCK'S EGG."

MYTHOLOGY IN VICTORIAN ART

Many of the Victorian artists involved in painting the nude came from the middle and upper classes. This being so, they went to schools where Latin and Greek were taught and were consequently exposed to classical mythology at the most impressionable age. The myths and legends of the past were familiar to them in a way it is almost impossible to conceive today. The same legends had been used as raw material by the great painters of the past, so even those artists who had come from humble stock were acquainted with Greek mythology (always more important than Roman) through seeing paintings on mythological subjects, or engravings of them. Painters such as Etty and Watts, who came from the artisan or the lower-middle classes, were mentally as well stocked with antique themes as those such as Lord Leighton and Alma-Tadema, who stemmed from the professional classes.

The most significant storehouse of myths came from ancient Greece. The characters of Greek mythology fall into three groups: the gods of Olympus and their consorts, divine or human; personifications of natural phenomena, such as the sun, the moon and the seasons; or heroes or heroines, who were mortal, but who could occasionally be elevated into gods. They usually had at least one immortal ancestor. From the third century BC Greek gods and goddesses were given new names to equate them with the Roman divinities. Generally, the Victorian artists used the Roman versions, and the Roman names are most often used below. To avoid confusion, the following lists the more common names, Latin first and then the Greek.

AESCULAPIUS	ASCLEPIUS	MARS	ARES
APOLLO	APOLLO	MERCURY	HERMES
BACCHUS	DIONYSUS	MINERVA	ATHENE
CERES	DEMETER	NEPTUNE	POSEIDON
CUPID	EROS	PARCAE (THE FATES)	MOERAE
DIANA	ARTEMIS	PLUTO	HADES
THE FURIES	ERINNYES	PROSERPINA	PERSEPHONE
THE GRACES	CHARITIES	SATURN	CRONUS
HERCULES	HERACLES	TELLUS	GAEA
JUNO	HERA	VENUS	APHRODITE
JUPITER	ZEUS	VESTA	HESTIA
LUNA	SELENE	VULCAN	HEPHAESTUS

Opposite Raphael Kirchner was the master of the saucy postcard and brought to the Edwardians a light-hearted naughtiness which always kept within the bounds of good taste (and thus ensured that his postcards were permitted through the post by the General Post Office). He, more than anyone, expresses the new spirit of the twentieth century before the Great War dashed its hopes.

Aegina
Carried off by Zeus in the likeness of an eagle (some say flame). Her father, the river-god Asopus, pursued them, vowing revenge, but was forced to return to the river-bed when Zeus blasted him with a thunderbolt. Other sources declare that, to avoid his wrath, Zeus turned her into an island and himself into a rock.

Alcmene
Zeus took advantage of the absence of Alcmene's husband to assume her husband's appearance and ravish her, and when the husband returned he was surprised by Alcmene's coolness. It was all explained later, however, by the soothsayer Teiresias.

Amazons
A race of warlike women, put to the sword by Hercules in one of his twelve labours. Amazons were occasionally used as subject-matter by Victorian artists, but more often by sculptors.

Andromache
The wife of Hector, who was killed in the Trojan Wars, while her son was hurled from the battlements. After capture she was allotted to Pyrrhus, son of Achilles, to whom she bore three children, and then she was passed on to someone else. Andromache was noted for her quiet dignity and resignation in the face of misfortune, qualities that endeared themselves to the Victorians, and she was frequently the subject chosen by artists, as well as by the playwrights Racine and Euripides.

Andromeda
Rescued by Perseus (q.v.) after being chained to a rock to await the arrival of a monster sent by Neptune.

Antigone
Antigone boasted that her hair was more beautiful than that of Juno, wife of Zeus, and in revenge Juno turned her hair into serpents.

Antiope
The sister of Aegina, Antiope, was ravished while she lay sleeping by Zeus in the form of a satyr.

Apollo
Sun-god, shepherd-god, Apollo was widely portrayed by artists of all ages as the epitome of male beauty, often equipped with a bow, a quiver, a shepherd's crook or a lyre.

Arachne
Arachne challenged the goddess Athene to compete with her in spinning. Athene could not find any fault in the girl's work and so turned her into a spider, destined to spin forever and to draw from her own body the material.

Arethusa
One of the Nereids who lived beneath the sea, pursued by the hunter Alpheius on to dry land, where she turned into a spring.

Ariadne
Ariadne's role was to provide Theseus with a ball of twine so that he could track the Minotaur through the labyrinth in which the creature lived and slay it.

Arthurian legend
Tennyson was the chief popularizer of Arthur and the Knights of the Round Table, and his view of the age of chivalry influenced the artists who used Arthurian legend. There was not a great opportunity for painters of the female nude, except in the case of knights errant rescuing damsels in distress. The somewhat self-conscious mediaevalism of William Morris and his circle also influenced artists towards the end of the century, and Arthurian legend found expression in the work of Burne-Jones.

Asteria
One of the many targets of Zeus's lust, evading him by turning herself into a quail and throwing herself into the sea, whereupon she became a floating island.

Although entitled *A Summer Night*, this picture by Albert
Moore, one of the more self-effacing Victorian High Art
painters, evokes the mythology of ancient Greece.

Athene (Minerva)

The warrior-goddess, frequently painted by
artists of every age, the daughter of Zeus
and Metis, whom Zeus swallowed as she
was about to give birth to Athene.
Complaining of a headache, Zeus agreed to
have his skull split open with an axe, and
Athene sprang from the gaping wound.
Athene was noted for her chastity, and
when Teiresias saw her bathing, Athene
blinded him. She later relented and gave
him the gift of soothsaying.

Atlanta

Athlete, hunter and slayer of Centaurs and
other monsters, Atlanta had something in
common with the goddess Diana. She
agreed to marry the man who could beat
her in a race. Melanion had three golden
apples given to him by Venus, and as he
raced with her, Atlanta picked them up,
and was thus beaten, and married
Melanion. They were later turned into lions
for no very clear reason.

Callisto

A companion of Diana, Callisto took a vow
of chastity, but Zeus approached her
pretending to be Diana, and before she
could realize the mistake he had ravished
her. While bathing with her companions,
Diana realized that Callisto was pregnant,
and to protect her from the goddess's rage
Zeus turned her into a bear. But Diana
killed the bear with her bow and arrow,
and Callisto died giving birth to a son.

Calypso

A nymph who offered hospitality to
Odysseus for seven years, and was
prevented from rendering him immortal by
order of Zeus.

Cassandra

Cassandra was often interpreted by painters
as an old hag, but there was no reason for
this. She was loved by Apollo, and so that
she would give in to him he promised her
the gift of prophecy. She refused to keep to
her bargain, but Apollo begged one kiss,

Abbey Altson was a prolific illustrator for *The Pall Mall Magazine* and echoes of Greek mythology are often found in this artist's work.

and when this was given breathed into her mouth so that although she kept the gift of prophecy he made certain that no one would believe her.

Castalia
In order to escape from the amorous intentions of Apollo, Castalia threw herself into a fountain which afterwards bore her name.

Centaurs
Creatures with the head and chest of a man and lower body and legs of a horse.

Ceres (Demeter)
Goddess of tillage and corn, Ceres was raped by Zeus and gave birth to Persephone (Proserpina).

The Chimaera
Daughter of Typhon, son of the spirit of the hurricane, the Chimaera had the head of a lion, the body of a goat, and the tail of a dragon. She billowed flames, and was the personification of the storm-cloud.

Circe
A daughter of Helios, Circe was enchantress and moon-goddess, building herself a palace on an island and turning all men who landed on the island into animals. She features in the *Odyssey*, where the companions of Odysseus (Ulysses) are turned into swine. Nevertheless Odysseus spent a year with her. She was a very popular subject for Victorian artists, as a fashionable vamp in mythological trappings.

Clytie
A mortal who cherished a passion for the god Helios (who personified the sun). Helios only had eyes for her sister, Leucothia, and, jealous, Clytie told their father who buried Leucothia alive. Helios returned in haste, but even his heat could not bring Leucothia back to life, so he changed her into an incense bush. Clytie died of despair, and her body took root in the soil. Her limbs changed to a stalk, her head into a flower, turned towards the sun (Helios). It was a theme that greatly appealed to Victorian artists.

Coronis
After yielding to Apollo and becoming pregnant, Coronis married someone else, and a crow left by Apollo to watch her returned to the god to tell him of the infidelity. In a rage, Apollo turned the plumage of the crow black, and put Coronis and her husband to death. On the funeral pyre Apollo snatched the child who was about to be born as Asclepius (in Latin, Aesculapius), god of healing.

Crenae (Pegae)
Nymphs of springs.

Cronus (Saturn)
Having with his mother, Gaea, reduced his father, Uranus, to impotence, Cronus carried on the work of creation. Among the

products of his dynasty were Momus (Gaiety), Oizus (Misery), the Fates and, a theme for Victorian artists, the Hesperides who guarded the golden apples beyond the Ocean. To Nereus and Doris, daughter of the Ocean, were born fifty daughters, the Nereids, widely used as subject matter for painters. In early Greek mythology there is little to differentiate gods, monsters and natural phenomena and forces, and all combine with one another to produce offspring, such as the Harpies. There was no difficulty in visualizing Harpies, but considerable effort was needed to personify the three thousand sons of Oceanus and Tethys, the Rivers. Cronus married his sister Rhea, who bore him three daughters, Hestia, Demeter and Hera (in Latin, Vesta, Ceres and Juno), and three sons, Hades, Poseidon and Zeus (in Latin, Pluto, Neptune and Jupiter). Fearful of being overthrown by his progeny, Cronus swallowed each of his children in turn, but his wife applied to their parents Uranus and Gaea for help, and Zeus was born in a cavern in Crete in secret, Cronus being given a stone wrapped in swaddling clothes as an imitation Zeus, which he duly swallowed. Later Zeus overthrew Cronus, and forced him to disgorge his brothers and sisters, who of course all became gods and goddesses.

Danae

Having been told by an oracle that his daughter would one day bear a son who would kill him, Danae's father imprisoned her in a chamber of bronze. Zeus had designs on Danae, and visited her in the form of a shower of gold, resulting in a son, Perseus. The father locked mother and child in a box, threw them into the sea, from where they were eventually rescued.

Daphne

Pursued by Apollo, Daphne was about to be caught by him and ravished, but she called for help from the venerable mother-goddess Gaea and the earth gaped open. From this opening a laurel tree sprang, and Apollo made it sacred to him.

Daphnis

Legendary hero of Sicilian shepherds, Daphnis was born of Mercury and a nymph, and was found by shepherds in a grove of laurels. In due course he had his own herd, which he tended while playing on his Pan-pipes. He won the affection of a nymph who made him promise to be true to her, but in this he failed, and he was smitten with blindness. He soon died, and changed into a rock or was wafted into heaven by Mercury. His name is usually associated with that of Chloë.

Dia

A little-known conquest by Zeus, who ravished her in the form of a horse.

Diana (Artemis)

Goddess of the hunt and forests, Diana has been widely depicted as an athletic young woman, especially by sculptors. Extremely chaste, she expected her companions to be likewise, and if they did not come up to her high standards she turned them into something or killed them. When bathing she was seen by Actaeon, whom she turned into a stag and had slaughtered by her hounds.

Dryads

Nymphs of the forest.

Echo

A nymph whose singing distracted Juno when her husband Zeus was in pursuit of some new conquest. Juno revenged herself by taking away Echo's speech, condemning her to repeat only the last syllable of others' words. Echo fell in love with Narcissus but, unable to say anything, she was ignored and died disconsolate, leaving only the echo of her voice.

Endymion

Best known on account of Keats's poem, Endymion asked Zeus to grant him immortality and eternal youth, and this was agreed on condition that Endymion enjoyed eternal sleep.

Eos (Aurora)

The personification of dawn, Eos was

interpreted as a winged goddess dispensing dew from an urn, sometimes mounted on the horse Pegasus, sometimes travelling in a horse-drawn chariot.

Eros (Cupid)
The youngest of the gods, a winged prankster whose darts and arrows inflamed passions, even those of his mother Venus. Perhaps the most often portrayed of all mythological creatures, in all mediums from Valentine cards to the statue of Eros in Piccadilly Circus.

Europa
Europa was one of the better known of Zeus's mates, approached by the god in the form of a bull. She caressed the bull and climbed on its back, upon which it raced away carrying off the girl.

Eurydice
Wife of Orpheus (q.v.) who died after being bitten by a snake and was pursued into the Underworld by her husband, but he was unable to bring her back.

The Fates (Moerae)
Three in number, they were Clotho, the spinner, symbolizing the thread of life, Lachesis, personifying luck, and Atropos, the destiny no man can avoid.

Flora
A modest Roman goddess, responsible for spring.

The Furies
The Furies sprang from the blood of Uranus after he had been castrated by Gaea and her son Cronus. They were Tisiphone, Alecto and Megaera, and are known collectively as goddesses of vengeance.

Gaea
In the beginning, wrote the poet Hesiod (eighth century BC), there was Chaos, a vast dark empty space, and then there appeared Gaea 'the deep-breasted earth', and Eros. Gaea bore Uranus, the sky, and then created the mountains and the sea. Gaea and Uranus united and bore the Titans, six male and six female, and the one-eyed Cyclopes, and then three monsters, whom Uranus shut up in the depths of the earth. Gaea mourned the monsters, and revenged herself on Uranus with the help of her son Cronus (Saturn), by castrating him. The blood turned into the Furies, to giants and to nymphs (the Meliae). The genitals floated on the surface of the sea and broke into white foam, from which was born the goddess Aphrodite (Venus). Gaea was not a character widely used by Victorian artists, but the myth itself explains Botticelli's *The Birth of Venus*. The Eros of this myth has little to do with the later god of love.

Galatea
One of the Nereids who was courted by the one-eyed giant Polyphemus. She was enamoured of Acis, a herdsman, whom Polyphemus crushed under a boulder. Galatea had Acis changed into a river for reasons best known to herself.

Ganymede
A mortal man of great beauty whom an eagle brought to Olympus, by order of Zeus. This myth was often painted.

The Graces
Part of Venus's retinue, who helped her with her toilet, and who were associated with spring, when they mingled with the nymphs and danced with them. They were a subject chosen by many Victorian artists, represented as nude from as early as the fourth century BC. The number of Graces varied according to convenience, but they were usually reckoned as three, Aglaia, Euphrosyne and Thalia, though their names were of no account as they were always a collective trio.

The Harpies
The Harpies, often associated with the Furies, have come down to us personified as rapacious filthy monsters, half-bird, half-woman, and also as a personification of the storm-wind. Their favourite habit was to devour food from tables, soiling with excrement that which they did not carry away. They were sometimes used by the

more gloomy Victorian artists, occasionally glamorized into *femmes fatales*.

Hebe
Daughter of Zeus and Juno, Hebe had the gift of eternal youth. Her main duty was handing round nectar and ambrosia to the gods. She once fell and accidentally exposed herself and was replaced by Ganymede.

Hecate
A goddess of enchantments and spells, haunting crossroads, tombs and horrid places.

The Heliads
The sisters of Phaethon, son of Helios, who had come to grief driving the sun's chariot and was struck down by Zeus with a thunderbolt to prevent him destroying the universe. The Heliads gathered by Phaethon's tomb and were changed to poplars, their tears becoming amber.

Hercules (Heracles)
A hero rather than a god, born of the union of Zeus and Amphitryon who, in a fit of madness wished on him by Juno, killed his wife and children, and had to atone by carrying out twelve gigantic tasks (the labours of Hercules).

Hermaphroditus
Bathing one day, Hermaphroditus was seen by the nymph Salmacis, who pursued him but was repulsed. In the struggle, Salmacis told him that his resistance was in vain, and nothing would separate them. Their two bodies fused as one.

Hesperides
The sisters who guarded in the garden to the west the golden apples received as a wedding present from her mother-in-law, Gaea, by Hera, on her marriage to Zeus.

The Horae
These young maidens personified the seasons and varied in number and purpose. They are usually depicted with corn, branches or vines in their hands or

Mediaeval chivalry features strongly in Tennyson and in the Pre-Raphaelite painters, of whom Millais was a founder-member. It is rare to find a nude in Millais, who became immensely famous through his pictures *Bubbles* and *Cherry Ripe*, but *A Knight Errant* exploits the Victorian interest in chained nude ladies.

garlanding someone. The most popular estimate of their number was three—Irene, Dike, and Eunomia.

Io
Taken by Zeus in the form of a cloud, but despite this ingenious trick Juno, the wife of Zeus, was suspicious, and Io was then turned into a heifer, and driven mad by a gad-fly sent by Juno to torment her. Fleeing, Io gave her name to the Ionian Sea, and was later restored by Zeus to human form.

Iris
Iris personified the rainbow and was also messenger of the gods, recognized by her golden wings, and hand-maiden to Juno. She was a minor multi-purpose goddess.

Juno (Hera)
Visited by Zeus in the likeness of a cuckoo. As the cuckoo seemed cold, Juno warmed

it at her breast, upon which Zeus assumed his normal form and took advantage of Juno on promise of marriage.

Leda
A very popular subject for painters of all ages, Leda was approached by Zeus in the form of a swan, seduced by him, and the same night lay with her husband. The four children she bore through this double mating were divided equally between Zeus and her husband.

Limnads
Nymphs of stagnant water.

Medusa
Neptune seduced Medusa in the shape of a horse or bird in the temple of Athene. Athene revenged herself by turning Medusa's hair into serpents. Medusa in due time was decapitated by Perseus, and the blood gave birth to Chrysaor and the horse Pegasus.

Mera
A companion of Diana, Mera was killed by her for having permitted herself to be ravished by Zeus.

Mercury (Hermes)
God of travellers and of commerce, Mercury was usually conceived with a winged helmet and winged sandals. Often depicted in paintings and sculpture, he had amorous adventures with Persephone, Hecate and Aphrodite, but these rarely found expression in the arts.

Metis (Wisdom)
The first wife of Zeus, who 'knew more things than all the gods and men put together'. Fearing overthrow by any offspring of this alliance, Zeus swallowed the mother and unborn child.

Mnemosyne
A wife of Zeus for nine nights, who eventually gave birth to the nine Muses.

The Muses
Besides being shepherd-god and sun-god, Apollo was god of music, and in this capacity he was attended by the Muses, nine in all, Clio, Euterpe, Thalia, Melpomene, Terpsichore, Erato, Polyhymnia, Urania and Calliope. They were originally spring nymphs, but later they were each given specific roles. As spring nymphs they were shy and chaste, but later they were less sparing of their charms, especially with Apollo.

Naiads
Nymphs of brooks, often used in Victorian paintings.

Narcissus
Having rejected the love of the nymph Echo, Narcissus was punished by the gods by having him fall in love with his own image. So infatuated was he by his reflection in water that he turned into the flower that bears his name.

Nausicaa
During his travels Odysseus was swept into the sea from a raft. He managed to swim to shore, where he was found by Nausicaa. She supplied him with clothes and took him to her father's palace where he was regally entertained. The incident of Odysseus and Nausicaa formed the subject of a lost play by Sophocles, and was often represented in both ancient and more modern art.

Nemesis
A somewhat hazy female goddess, symbolizing divine anger at mortal transgressions.

Neptune (Poseidon)
The sea-god, associated with Gaea, Ceres (who changed into a mare to escape him—Neptune then changed into a stallion), Tyro and Medusa, among many others. He did not greatly interest artists.

The Nereids
Fifty virgins who lived with their father, Nereus, below the sea and were sometimes seen on the surface.

Themis and Eos. At a lower level again were the Horae, the Moerae, Nemesis, the Graces, the Muses, Iris, Hebe and Ganymede.

Oreads
Nymphs of mountains and grottoes.

Orion
Orion is believed to have been one of the few males, gods or men, on whom the goddess Diana had her eye. When Orion was swimming one day Diana's brother, Apollo, invited her to shoot an arrow at a distant speck. This she did, and killed Orion. Another version has Orion touching the goddess when they were out hunting together, with Diana being so affronted that she summoned a scorpion to sting Orion.

Orpheus
Noted for his gift for music, Orpheus was occasionally used as a subject by artists in association with his wife, the nymph Eurydice. She died after being bitten by a snake and Orpheus followed her into the Underworld to get her back. Pluto and his consort agreed to let her return if Orpheus did not look back at her, but this he did, and Eurydice vanished forever.

Oyane
A nymph who accompanied Persephone when carried off by Pluto to the underworld, and who turned herself into a fountain after Persephone had gone.

Pan
The shepherd-god, with the legs, horns and beard of a goat, who frolicked through the woods and chased nymphs, including Syrinx, who turned into a reed to avoid his attentions. Pan made the reeds into a musical instrument, the Pan-pipes.

Pandora
Pandora, the first woman, was created by Hephaestus (Vulcan) from clay and water under instructions from Zeus so that through her he could revenge himself on Man for the theft by Prometheus of

The legend of Perseus and Andromeda inspired many Victorian painters of the nude, but none so powerfully as Lord Leighton in this dramatic realization. The model is Dorothy Dene and the landscape was based on sketches Leighton made in 1874 in Donegal. The picture dates from 1891.

Nymphs
Creatures of wood and mountain, their main role was to be pursued by Pan, Zeus and other divinities.

Olympians
The gods assembled on Mount Olympus and formed their own society, headed by the twelve premier gods and goddesses: Zeus, Poseidon, Hephaestus, Hermes, Ares and Apollo were the male; Hera, Athene, Artemis, Hestia, Aphrodite and Demeter were the female. Beneath them were Helios, Selene, Leto, Dione, Dionysus,

heavenly fire. Pandora had a box—some say vase—which contained all the ills of human life. Except for hope, they all escaped, and spread over the earth.

Pasiphae
Wife of King Minos of Crete. Neptune, being annoyed by Minos, inspired Pasiphae with love of a bull, and the union resulted in the Minotaur.

Persephone (Proserpine)
Wife of Pluto (Hades) the ruler of the Underworld, sometimes called Kore, snatched away by Pluto from the surface as she was gathering flowers.

Perseus
The progeny of Zeus and Danae (whom Zeus ravished in the guise of a shower of gold). He slew Medusa, and intervened between Neptune and the King of Ethiopia, Cepheus. The wife of the king had claimed that she was more beautiful than the Nereids, and Neptune had sent a monster as an answer to this impudence. An oracle declared that the country could be saved only by sacrificing the king's daughter, Andromeda, to the monster, so she was chained to a rock to await death. Perseus arrived, fell in love with her, and killed the monster. Perseus married Andromeda, and from this union there arose a dynasty of heroes, the most important of which was Hercules. The Perseus and Andromeda theme was a popular one with Victorian artists (particularly as the Victorians liked to see a naked woman chained to a rock).

Potamids
Nymphs of rivers and streams.

Psyche
A princess of such beauty that Venus was jealous of her, so much so that Eros was summoned to teach Psyche a lesson. An oracle ordered Psyche's father to conduct Psyche to the top of a mountain where she was to be the victim of a monster. Resignedly Psyche waited, but she was suddenly wafted by Zephyrus to a palace.

She fell asleep, to be awakened by a mysterious stranger who told her that he was her destined husband. Forbidding her ever to try and see his face, the stranger disappeared at dawn, returning every night. Fearing that she was shackled to a monster, Psyche lit a lamp, and found that her husband was Eros. Hot oil fell on Eros as he slept, and he awoke, reproached Psyche, and disappeared, together with the palace, leaving Psyche on a lonely rock. Attempting suicide, she threw herself into a nearby river, but was carried to the opposite bank. She was pursued vengefully by Venus, but Eros interceded, applied to Zeus for help and Psyche was made immortal and wedded to Eros. The story provided material for many artists.

Satyrs
Personifications of woods and mountains, sensual, part-goat, part-monkey, faithful companions of the gods whom they amused at festivals.

Scandinavian legend
Not surprisingly, considering the climate, the legends of Scandinavia as transcribed by William Morris did not fire those Victorian artists who specialized in the depiction of nude figures.

Selene
Selene was the sister of the sun-god Helios, and after his daily journey across the sky she took over, riding in the sky on her horse-drawn chariot, or mounted on a bull, mule, or horse. She was loved by Zeus, Pan in the form of a white ram, and Endymion. Endymion asked Zeus to confer immortality and eternal youth on him. Zeus agreed on condition that Endymion enjoyed eternal sleep.

Semele
One of the less well known of Zeus's conquests, Semele was the target of Juno's jealousy. Juno came to her rival in disguise, and tempted her to ask Zeus to appear before her undisguised, in all his majesty and glory. Zeus tried to dissuade Semele,

without avail, and when he came to her in his chariot, accompanied by thunder and lightning, the spectacle killed her, and she was consumed by fire. Zeus gathered up the child she carried in her womb and placed it in his thigh until it was time for it to be born. The child was Dionysus (Bacchus).

The Sirens
The Sirens could be half-bird, half-woman, but were most often depicted as women with fish-tails, usually carrying a lyre and luring men with their sweet voices. Their numbers ranged from two to eight, depending on which mythology, and in Victorian art they were largely associated with the *Odyssey*. Sometimes they were depicted as glamorous nudes.

Taygete
A somewhat shadowy figure who was turned into a hind by Diana when being pursued by Zeus.

Themis
Daughter of Uranus and Gaea, Themis gave order to the world. She gave birth to the Horae (Seasons), Eunomia (Wise Law), Dike (Justice), Eirene (Peace) and the Moerae (the Fates). After her replacement (as consort of Zeus), Themis continued to live on Olympus and was widely respected.

Theseus
A destroyer of monsters, Theseus is best known for his exploit in killing the Minotaur. After being provided with a ball of twine by Ariadne, he was able to find his way through the labyrinth in which the Minotaur lived.

Thetis
The most famous of the submarine Nereids was Thetis, sought in marriage by both Zeus and Neptune on account of her beauty, but eventually given by Zeus to a mortal. She tried to escape this by changing into a fish, an animal, a wave and a flame, all to no avail. She bore Achilles, and to make him invulnerable held him in the River Styx by the heel, which of course was

unprotected, and in due course gave the English language the phrase 'Achilles heel'.

The Tritons
Half-men, half-fish, some with horses' legs, some blowing conch shells, the Tritons sometimes feature as background interest in Victorian paintings depicting mermaids or the Nereids.

Tyro
Seduced by Neptune in the guise of a river-god.

Uranus
Mate of Gaea, the primitive earth-mother, castrated by their son Cronus.

Venus (Aphrodite)
By far the most important of the mythological personages to people the canvases of the Victorian artists. Her sensuality was emphasized by the Greek sculptors (who used prostitutes as their models). She was the daughter of the primary mother-figure, Gaea, and Uranus, who was castrated by their son Cronus in alliance with Gaea. Venus arose from the foam of the severed genitals floating in the sea. Her presence on Olympus was not welcomed by all, and at a wedding reception a golden apple was tossed into the hall bearing the description *For the fairest*. Venus, Juno (Hera) and Athene (Minerva) all claimed it and to solve the problem Zeus invited a mortal, Paris, to judge. Venus loosened her robes and promised Paris the most beautiful of women (who turned out to be Helen of Troy), She won. This is the Judgment of Paris, often used as a subject by artists of every age. Venus took as husband the ugliest of her suitors, Vulcan (Hephaestus). Her lovers included Adonis, Phaethon and Mars (Ares). Her son, Hermaphroditus, was fathered by Mercury. Another son was Eros.

Vesta (Hestia)
Goddess of fire and domestication, Vesta was chaste, immobile, and rather shadowy, but she appealed to the Victorians, and

Henry Ryland was a somewhat disillusioned
artist who complained bitterly that the public
only wanted pretty-pretty paintings. It was the
type of work that suited his talents though, as is
clear from this picture called *The Young Orpheus*.

Vesta became not only the name of a match
but a popular Christian name (for example,
Vesta Tilley and Vesta Victoria).

Water Nymphs
Every spring, brook, river and pool had
resident divinities who sometimes lived in
the water, sometimes nearby, spinning and
weaving. They occasionally mixed with
more exalted personages. Always young
and beautiful, the nymphs could pull down
mortals into their waters, but were basically
lovable creatures.

Zeus
The most important of the Greek deities,
the son of Cronus and Rhea, who fought
the forces of disorder and upheaval and
provided the artists of the Victorian period
with an unending supply of material,
mainly related to his curious and turbulent
love life.

Acknowledgements

The author and publishers are grateful to the following for permission to reproduce copyright illustrations: Michael S. Alexander: 72; E.T. Archives Ltd: 153, 157, 159, (Leighton House) 35 (left), 54, (Royal Academy) 53; Fine Art Society: 61, 65, 70, 85, 113, 114, 127, 129; La Galleria Nazionale d'Arte Moderna, Rome: 71 (below); Hessisches Landesmuseum, Darmstadt: 142 (above); Private Collection, formerly in the collection of R.H. Benson: 105; Sotheby's, Belgravia: 17, 18, 21, 23, 28, 36, 38, 56, 58, 59, 67, 71 (above), 93, 94, 97, 101, 104, 106, 122, 150.

INDEX

Page numbers in italic type refer to illustrations.